Guide
Prehistoric
Ruins
of the
Southwest

NORMAN T. OPPELT

PRUETT *P* PUBLISHING COMPANY
Boulder, Colorado

First Edition

4   5   6   7   8   9

Printed in the United States of America

Library of Congress Cataloging in Publication Data

Oppelt, Norman T.
  Guide to prehistoric ruins of the Southwest.

  Bibliography: p.
  "Archaeological Resources Protection Act of
1979": p.
  1. Indians of North America—Southwest, New—Antiq-
uities. 2. Excavations (Archaeology)—Southwest, New.
3. Southwest, New—Antiquities. I. United States.
Archaeological Resources Protection Act of 1979. 1981.
II. Title. III. Title: Prehistoric ruins of the Southwest.
E78.S7066   978   81-5156
ISBN 0-87108-587-9   AACR2

Acknowledgments

I am indebted to a number of persons who aided in the gathering of information and production of this guide. Foremost was the encouragement and support given to me by my wife, Pat, and our children, Eric and Karen who accompanied me on nearly all of my visits to prehistoric ruins over the past decade. Their interest and patience are appreciated, and made my work much more enjoyable. I also want to thank Mae and Waldo Bast who tolerated the interruptions in their plans when I needed to stop at a ruin or spend time in a library on our trips to Arizona.

Avocational archeologists who provided assistance and encouragement over the years included Charles McLain, Greeley, Colorado; Jack French, Ft. Collins, Colorado; Franklin and Joan Barnett, Prescott, Arizona; George Kelly, Cortez, Colorado; Richard Ellison, Silver City, New Mexico; Bill Sundt, Albuquerque, New Mexico; Charles Brougher, Pleasant View, Colorado; and Don and Shirley Hill, Greeley, Colorado.

Several professional archeologists also gave me assistance and advice concerning this guide. Among these were George Fay, University of Northern Colorado; Watson Smith, Tucson, Arizona; Al Lancaster, Cortez, Colorado; Bruce Rippeteau and Ray Lyons, Denver, Colorado; David Doyel, Window Rock, Arizona; Sharon Urban, Arizona State Museum, Tucson; Evelyn Ely and Curtis Schaafsma, Laboratory of Anthropology, Santa Fe, New Mexico; Charles DiPeso, Amerind Foundation, Dragoon, Arizona; Katharine Bartlett and Donald Weaver, Museum of Northern Arizona, Flagstaff; Robert Euler, Grand Canyon National Park; and Joe Ben Wheat and Dave Breternitz, University of Colorado, Boulder.

My thanks are also given to the library staffs of the following institutions who willingly gave their time and expertise to help me find written materials: University of Northern Colorado, Greeley; Colorado State University, Ft. Collins; University of Colorado, Boulder; Laboratory of Anthropology, Santa Fe, New Mexico; and Museum of Northern Arizona, Flagstaff. I also want to express my appreciation to the many federal and state park service personnel who gave me directions and patiently answered my questions. These unnamed persons dedicate their efforts to maintaining and protecting our archeological heritage so it may be enjoyed and studied. It is evident that without their commitment and the governmental resources there would be little remaining of the fascinating prehistoric cultures of the Southwest.

To all others who were involved in the planning, writing, and production of this guide, I give my appreciation and congratulations for a job well done.

Ted Oppelt
Greeley, Colorado

Contents

Map Legend

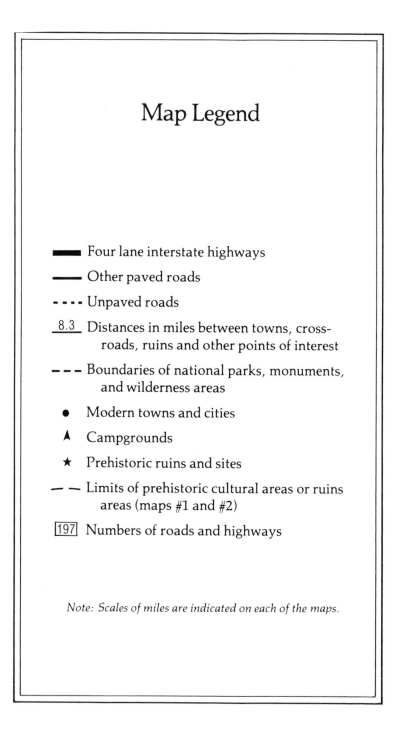

▬▬ Four lane interstate highways

── Other paved roads

- - - - Unpaved roads

<u>8.3</u> Distances in miles between towns, cross-
roads, ruins and other points of interest

– – – Boundaries of national parks, monuments,
and wilderness areas

● Modern towns and cities

▲ Campgrounds

★ Prehistoric ruins and sites

– — Limits of prehistoric cultural areas or ruins
areas (maps #1 and #2)

197 Numbers of roads and highways

Note: Scales of miles are indicated on each of the maps.

Preface

The ruins of ancient cultures hold a fascination for modern man, and much has been written about the great sites in Egypt, Greece, India, and Meso-America. For those who can visit them in person, or for the armchair traveler who must experience them through the words and pictures of others, these areas can provide much learning and enjoyment. These faraway places are quite well known, either firsthand or vicariously, to many Americans.

What many people do not realize is that some of the most interesting prehistoric ruins and primitive arts exist right in our own Southwest. This area extends roughly from the Pecos River on the east to the Colorado River on the west and includes southwestern Colorado and southern Utah on the north. To the south, this cultural area extends into the northern parts of the Mexican states of Sonora and Chihuahua. This is a region of great natural contrasts, including hot, arid deserts, cool, forested mountains, and some of the most spectacular canyons and scenery in the world.

The Southwest can be visited by those who either want to stay in the comfort of modern motels or by those who, out of preference or necessity, want to camp and prepare their own meals. Over the past ten years, my family and I have visited many of the major sites covered in this guide. In most cases, we camped in our pickup or stayed in inexpensive motels. Preparing our own breakfasts and lunches and eating out for some dinners proved to be an economical way to visit the ruins, museums, and other points of interest. We found this an enjoyable family experience in these days when many families seem to be losing their cohesiveness.

We discovered that children prefer the ruins where they can be

1

active and not just look. They like to climb the ladders and enter rooms and caves at such places as Bandelier, Mesa Verde, and Kiet Siel. The horseback trips at Canyon de Chelly and Kiet Siel are especially popular. Small children are happiest when they have playmates their own age, so this should be kept in mind when making plans or choosing a campsite. You also should remember that the attention span of small children is rather short, which means that visiting museums, attending lectures, and looking at scenic views will not be their favorite activities. Fortunately, visiting most ruins involves at least some walking and/or climbing that gives everyone some good exercise.

Today, handicapped persons are being given greater consideration regarding their participation in a wider range of activities. My friendship with several disabled individuals has made me aware of the many barriers that prevent them from doing what the rest of us take for granted. Therefore, this guide will also indicate which ruins are accessible to those who cannot climb or who are confined to wheelchairs. Unfortunately, many of the ruins are not accessible to the handicapped. It is hoped that this book will encourage more disabled persons to visit the sites which they can see and that planners will consider removing barriers in future restoration and construction of facilities. By law, all projects using federal funds must provide for the handicapped, which means that more sites should become accessible in the future. In most restored ruins, a person in a wheelchair can get at least an overview, but steps or rough trails may prevent a closer view.

The purpose of this guide is to inform the reader about the prehistoric ruins of the Southwest and to make visits easier and more enjoyable. Other books related to this subject are listed in the bibliography. Several of these are particularly recommended. *Southwest Indian Country*, a Sunset Travel Book, is a good general guide to the region. It includes information on auto exploring, arts and crafts, tribal festivals, and sights. Another book, *America's Ancient Treasures* by Franklin Folsom, covers archeological sites and museums across the country, including some described in this guide. For those who want to camp in the Southwest, *Camping with the Indians* by Lowenkopf and Katz is helpful.

Some of the major ruins areas, such as Mesa Verde, Canyon de Chelly, and Bandelier, have been well publicized and adequately covered in other written materials; therefore, it is unnecessary to repeat a detailed description here. Rather, I have emphasized the lesser known sites, some of which are unrestored but nevertheless are interesting and archeologically significant. Few of these ruins have been described in recent publications.

Many archeological sites have been assigned numbers by various archeological institutions and researchers who have worked in the Southwest. Because a considerable number of sites are unnamed, and because several sites may have the same name, numbers help to avoid confusion. In many cases throughout this guide, these numbers are given in parentheses after the name of the site to assist the reader in obtaining additional information. The most commonly used initials and the institutions or individuals that they represent are listed below.

LA—Laboratory of Anthropology, Santa Fe
GP—Gila Pueblo, Globe, Arizona
ASM—Arizona State Museum, Tucson
NA—Museum of Northern Arizona, Flagstaff
RB—Rainbow Bridge Expedition
FB—Franklin Barnett
(CDC and CDM refer to Canyon de Chelly and Canyon del Muerto in Canyon de Chelly National Monument)

In addition to the maps in this guide, other maps will be useful to persons visiting prehistoric ruins and sites in the southwestern United States. The U. S. Geological Survey provides quadrangle maps with a scale of 1 to 250,000. These are very useful in locating the ruins and sites included in this guide. A list of these inexpensive maps may be obtained by writing to the U.S. Geological Survey, Denver, Colorado 80225. Maps of the national forests in this region are also of some use, but few prehistoric sites are specifically located on them. These maps may be obtained from the appropriate forest service headquarters or from the regional offices in Denver or Albuquerque. The state of Utah has produced a good map of the southeastern portion of the state where most of the major ruins are located. This multipurpose map may be purchased from the Utah Travel Council, Council Hall, Salt Lake City, Utah 84114. Multipurpose area maps are also available for Arizona. The source of these maps in Arizona is the Arizona Office of Tourism, 1700 West Washington, Phoenix, Arizona 85007. The scale of these maps is one inch equals five miles.

One of the best maps for visiting ruins in the Southwest is produced by the Automobile Club of Southern California, 2601 South Figueroa Street, Los Angeles, California. This map, known as

Indian Country (Map 2437), is not for sale to the public but is available to members of the American Automobile Association. Nonmembers may find a friend who belongs to this organization and will obtain a copy for them. This map covers the northwestern portion of the Southwest as far south as Prescott, Arizona, and east to Santa Fe, New Mexico. Unfortunately, to my knowledge, no comparable maps are available that cover the southern portion of the Southwest.

It should be stated also that unauthorized excavation of sites, collection of artifacts, or any disturbance of prehistoric remains is *not* permissible. At many sites, much valuable information has been lost due to such vandalism. Federal and state laws forbid digging, removing cultural objects, or destroying sites on government or Indian lands. In 1979, the Archeological Resources Protection Act was signed into law and several persons have been prosecuted for violating this law in southwestern states. The full text of this law is presented in Appendix I of this guide. In addition to the loss of scientific knowledge that results from site destruction, this activity robs the public of the opportunity to enjoy future accurate restorations and artifact exhibitions with their valuable provenience and catalog data.

Readers who may want to participate in excavations and learn more about archeology are encouraged to contact the museums, local associations, and educational institutions mentioned in this guide. Most of these organizations sponsor field schools, programs, or workshops in which avocational archeologists can work and learn under the supervision of qualified persons.

An organization named Earthwatch is a clearinghouse for expeditions and projects all over the world. In 1978, the opportunities to join archeological digs in the Southwest included a Mogollon site on the WS Ranch in the San Francisco Valley of New Mexico and the Salmon Ruins, an Anasazi pueblo in northwestern New Mexico. The address of Earthwatch is 10 Juniper Road, Box 127, Belmont, Massachusetts 02178.

Several southwestern states have or are establishing programs to certify nonprofessionals as archeological technicians or assistants. The layman who successfully completes the required program and examinations can be certified in such skills as surveying, excavation, or laboratory analysis of artifacts. A few professional archeologists are unwilling to cooperate with amateurs, but most generously give of their time to assist amateur societies and hopefully decrease the vandalization of prehistoric sites.

4

A number of sites included in this guide are located on private land. Persons wishing to visit these sites should *always* contact the owner or tenant and obtain permission to visit. A few land owners, usually because of previous vandalism, are not willing to permit any visits, but most, if asked politely and assured that no destruction will occur, are willing to give limited permission. It should also be noted that land may change ownership at any time, which may affect the availability of the sites.

The exact locations of unprotected sites are purposely not given in this guide. Readers are discouraged from visiting these sites unless they have permission from the private land owner or the federal land manager in the case of federal lands. In all of the geographical areas covered, there are at least a few protected sites that have been excavated and restored. These sites are of more interest to most visitors. The protected areas contain over 100 restored ruins, and most of these are described in this guide. Readers are strongly encouraged to visit these sites and to support the protection of all our archeological resources for future generations. Detailed directions are given to these sites, and they are marked by an asterisk. A good rule while visiting these ruins is, "Leave only footprints and take only photographs."

Norman T. Oppelt
January 1981

Map 1

Major Cultures of the Prehistoric Southwest

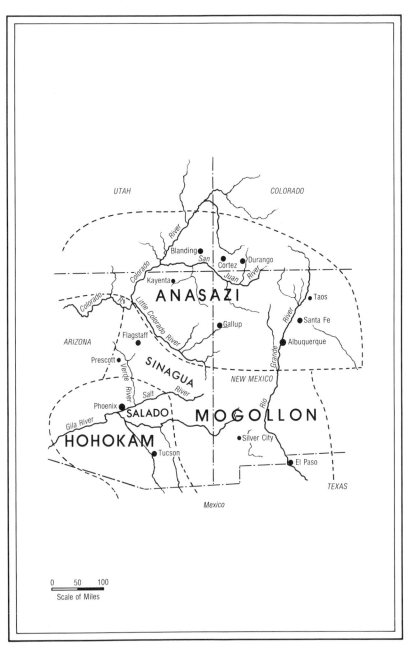

I

Introduction

Cultural Regions of the Southwest

Archeologists have categorized the prehistoric peoples of the Southwest into three major cultural regions: the Anasazi, the Mogollon, and the Hohokam. Each of these cultures has been divided into branches and/or geographical districts, some of which are mentioned in this guide. The geographical boundaries of these regions are shown in Map #1.

The Anasazi

The major portion of the prehistoric Southwest was inhabited by a cultural group known as the Anasazi. The Navajo word "anasazi" means "enemy ancestors" and refers to the ancestors of the present pueblo Indians of the northern Southwest. This wide-ranging culture extended over northern Arizona and New Mexico, southern Utah, and the southwestern corner of Colorado.

This large region has been divided into six major branches based on cultural characteristics within geographical areas. The first of these is the Mesa Verde branch. It covers the Four Corners area in the San Juan River drainage and extends west to where the San Juan River flows into the Colorado and east to the Piedra River. Mesa Verdans were also present in the Canyonlands area of southeastern Utah and in Canyon de Chelly in northeastern Arizona.

The Chaco branch centers on the large group of ruins in Chaco Canyon in northwestern New Mexico and extends in a westerly direction to the present New Mexico–Arizona state line. To the north, it reaches the San Juan River and includes the Salmon Ruins near Bloomfield, New Mexico.

The most easterly branch of the Anasazi is the Rio Grande, in the northern portion of the Rio Grande drainage. This region covers the drainage from the Taos area south to approximately the Rio Puerco of the West. From east to west, it reaches from Grants, New Mexico, to Pecos Pueblo, the most easterly of the major pueblo ruins.

The Little Colorado branch includes the upper portion of the Little Colorado River drainage in east-central Arizona and west-central New Mexico. It extends east into the Zuni area, north to the vicinity of Klagetoh Ruins, and west to near Flagstaff, Arizona. It is sparsely settled and the least studied of the Anasazi regions.

The sixth branch is known as the Virgin or Western Kayenta. The Virgin River lies in southwestern Utah. This branch covers the area often known as the Arizona Strip north of the Grand Canyon in Arizona and southwestern Utah north to the vicinity of the Coombs Site near Boulder, Utah. It also extends into the southeastern corner of Nevada near Las Vegas and includes Pueblo Grande de Nevada (Lost City) near Overton, Utah, most westerly of the major pueblo sites.

These branches have been determined by archeologists to describe and study the large Anasazi region, but it should not be assumed that there are definite boundaries or exclusive traits. As with the time periods, the branches phase into each other with some overlap, and many sites have features of one or more branches.

The Anasazi culture has also been divided into time periods based on cultural characteristics. These periods were first proposed in 1927, and, although they have been somewhat revised in recent years, they are still useful in understanding the development of this culture. The periods, their approximate dates, and a few of the major characteristics are as follows:

Basketmaker II, 100 B.C. to A.D. 500. Most Anasazi during this period lived in caves in shelters built of poles and mud. Pits were dug into the cave floors to store food, and burials were made in similar floor cists. Anasazi agriculture was initiated during this time with the cultivation of small amounts of corn. It is believed that corn was infused from people to the south, because it was known in Mexico long before it was utilized by the Anasazi. The Basketmaker II people were primarily hunters and gatherers. The bow and arrow had not yet been introduced in this area, and hunting was done with spears and spear throwers; animals were also trapped. Pottery making, which was already practiced by the Hohokam to the south, was not yet known to the Anasazi. The term "basketmaker" was first used by Richard Wetherill, who was one of the first to recognize that the remains which lay below the later pueblo materials indicated an earlier culture. The basketmakers were named for the expertly woven baskets found in their caves. Because few architectural remains of this culture exist today except in a few scattered caves, this guide includes very little related to this early period.

Basketmaker III, A.D. 500 to 700. This period provides the first material remains of major interest to visitors. These ruins include small villages of semisubterranean, circular structures known as pithouses. Agriculture intensified during these centuries, and beans, in addition to corn, were cultivated. People began to live together in larger groups, and the more efficient bow and arrow were introduced. Pottery of plain gray and later gray with black designs was developed. The more sedentary life during this time made pottery more practical, although fine baskets were still produced. A few Basketmaker III sites are included in this guide. Although little remains today except circular pithouse depressions, some of the sites described are: Shabik'eshchee Village in Chaco Canyon, several mesatop sites at Mesa Verde National Park, and Bear Ruin in the White Mountains of Arizona.

Pueblo I, A.D. 700 to 900. During this period, surface rooms grouped in small house blocks were constructed. Pithouses continued to be built and grew in size and complexity as the Anasazi became more sedentary. Pottery types became more variable, and black-on-white types became common. Black-on-red types were also produced in some areas, and some of the gray utility ware had a few unsmoothed coils around the necks of jars. Agriculture continued to improve and become more important, allowing the people to live together in larger villages. Pueblo I sites included in

Map 2
Prehistoric Ruins Areas of the Southwest

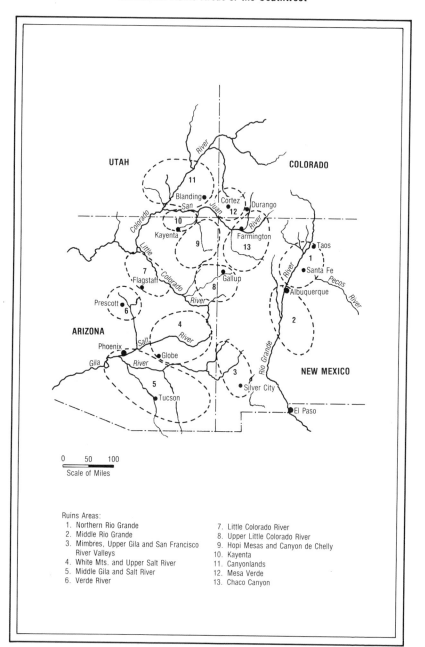

0   50   100
Scale of Miles

Ruins Areas:
1. Northern Rio Grande
2. Middle Rio Grande
3. Mimbres, Upper Gila and San Francisco
   River Valleys
4. White Mts. and Upper Salt River
5. Middle Gila and Salt River
6. Verde River

7. Little Colorado River
8. Upper Little Colorado River
9. Hopi Mesas and Canyon de Chelly
10. Kayenta
11. Canyonlands
12. Mesa Verde
13. Chaco Canyon

10

this guide are Piedra Ruin, White Mound Village, and Cahone Site #1.

Pueblo II, A.D. 900 to 1150. Population increased more rapidly in the Anasazi region during this time. The villages grew in size with surface rooms built in blocks of up to twenty-five rooms. Large, partly subterranean rooms that were probably used for religious ceremonies were present in most villages. It is believed that these rooms developed into the well-known kivas of later stages. Corrugated pottery with indented coils became a common utility ware over almost all of the Anasazi region. Black-on-white and black-on-red types continued as the most common decorated pottery. Some of the many Pueblo II sites included in this guide are Chetro Ketl, Hungo Pavie, and Una Vida in Chaco Canyon; Lowry Ruin; and King's Ruin.

Pueblo III, A.D. 1150 to 1300. This is sometimes referred to as the classic period of pueblo development. The Anasazi came together from small villages and built large masonry pueblos of several stories, some housing as many as 1,200 persons. Architecture and arts were developed to the highest level of prehistoric times. Beautiful polychrome pottery was made in some areas, and black-on-white types reached the zenith of their artistic and technical development. Trade with Hohokam, Mogollon, and other peoples to the south and west increased.

In the later part of this period, an exodus from this area occurred, and by the end of the thirteenth century, most of the Mesa Verde area and parts of the Kayenta and Chaco areas were almost entirely abandoned. The reasons for this move have been hotly debated by archeologists, but there has been little consensus. Reasons suggested have most commonly been a drought of twenty-five years, arroyo cutting that caused a decrease in flood irrigation, and pressure from hostile nomadic neighbors. Most of the northern Anasazi moved to the less-populated areas of central Arizona, west-central New Mexico, and the northern Rio Grande. Many of the major ruins included in this guide were built, inhabited, and abandoned during this period.

Pueblo IV, A.D. 1300 to 1598. This is considered by some to be a regressive period in the art and architecture of the Anasazi. In spite of evidence to support this point of view, there were still some well-built structures in the south, and in some areas, beautiful polychrome pottery was still being produced. Kivas continued to be important, and some of them, such as those at Pottery Mound,

11

Kuaua, and Awatovi, had fine murals. The initial Spanish contact with some of the Anasazi occurred in 1540, when Coronado entered the area of the northern Rio Grande. However, it was not until settlers began to arrive in 1598 that the Anasazi culture began to be significantly affected. In the seventeenth century, the Spanish had a great influence on the Rio Grande branch and to a lesser extent on the people in the Little Colorado and Kayenta areas. Some groups on the periphery of the Spanish settlement, such as the Hopis, were able to resist the Spanish religious and political pressures.

Kivas were used by most of the Anasazi branches from Pueblo III times onward. Kivas were round, or less commonly square, subterranean ceremonial rooms that also served as men's club rooms. Kivas often had a ventilator, a fire pit in front of the ventilator, and a deflector in between these two. It was common for kivas to have a small hole in the floor in line with the fire pit and ventilator. Known as the sipapu, this was the place of emergence of man from the underworld in the Pueblo creation myth. Kivas also usually had an interior bench around the perimeter of the chamber and four to eight masonry columns or pilasters, which supported the timbers of the cribbed roof. Entrance to the kiva was gained by a ladder through a hole in the center of the roof. This opening also served as a smoke escape. Kivas had no windows or doors and were quite dark without a fire for light.

Another related development in Anasazi architecture was the initiation of the ceremonial structure known as the great kiva. Nineteen of these structures have been fully or partially excavated. The earliest was built during the Basketmaker III period, but the great majority are from the Pueblo III era. Great kivas have been found in the Chaco, Mesa Verde, and Kayenta areas. The greatest concentration of these unusual ceremonial chambers is in Chaco Canyon, where eight of them are present. The most northerly known great kiva is at Lowry Ruin in southwestern Colorado, but great kivas also are present south to the Village of the Great Kivas near Zuni, New Mexico. Juniper Cove near Kayenta, Arizona, is the farthest west of these structures, while none are found further east than those in Chaco Canyon.

Great kivas vary in diameter from 33 feet 7 inches (Chetro Kettle III) to 81 feet (Ackmen). The average diameter of those studied is 49.7 feet.

Except for the fact that they are all subterranean and almost all are circular and have a bench, great kivas vary considerably in fea-

Partially restored Great Kiva, Lowry Ruin

tures. Masonry or timber roof supports, usually four in number, have been found in 89.5 percent of the great kivas studied. Other common features are raised fire boxes (63.2 percent); two floor vaults (57.9 percent); and a north antechamber (47.4 percent). All of these characteristics are more common in the later Pueblo III great kivas. Less common traits are a double bench (36.9 percent); wall crypts (31.6 percent); a fire screen (26.3 percent); and a sipapu (15.8 percent).

The only great kiva that has been completely restored is the one at Aztec Ruin. Others restored except for the roof are located at Lowry Ruin, Casa Rinconada, Pueblo Bonito, Chetro Kettl, and Fire Temple (at Mesa Verde National Park).

The Fremont culture east of the Colorado River in southern Utah is located north of the Anasazi region. This culture has a number of characteristics of the Anasazi and is considered by some to be a peripheral group to the more highly developed main Anasazi. Some of the northern sites in this guide are considered to be Fremont.

The Hohokam

The major prehistoric culture in the desert area of southcentral Arizona has been given the name Hohokam. The word Hohokam is a Pima Indian term meaning "those who have vanished."

Study of the remains of these ancient desert farmers has revealed much information about their life-style. Archeologists have divided the development of Hohokam culture into four time periods, with each period being further subdivided into two or more phases. The time periods and their dates are as follows:

Classic period—A.D. 1100 to 1450
Sedentary period—A.D. 900 to 1100
Colonial period—A.D. 550 to 900
Pioneer period—A.D. 300 to 550

These periods are useful for purposes of description and study, but one period phases into the next, and no abrupt cultural changes mark one period from the succeeding one.

The two main groups of the Hohokam have become known as the Desert Hohokam and the Riverine Hohokam. The Riverine Hohokam inhabited the middle Gila and lower Salt and lower Verde valleys. They were a desert agricultural people who, during the Pioneer period, planted crops near the Gila River and depended upon seasonal flooding to irrigate their fields. During the Pioneer period, relatively few Hohokam occupied the Salt and Verde River valleys, because those valleys did not lend themselves to flood irrigation. During the early part of the Colonial period, the concept of canal irrigation was introduced, probably from Mexico, causing a move into the Salt River area and a population increase.

Irrigation canals became an important factor in the development of the Hohokam culture and permitted the growth of large villages in the Gila Valley. There may have been as many as 250 miles of canals in the vicinity of the great villages near what is now the Phoenix metropolitan area. All of these were dug by hand, and the major canals were quite deep and wide. Remains of canals can be seen at Pueblo Grande in Phoenix. The Hohokam built the largest prehistoric irrigation system in North America, which enabled them to survive and prosper in a very dry climate.

Twenty-two large communities were located in the middle Gila Valley during the Classic period. These villages were composed of semisubterranean pithouses excavated below the ground level with the upper walls built of poles and the roofs covered with mud. Some of the villages also contained large earthen platform mounds and excavated ball courts, both of which were present in Mexico. Preparation of food and most other work was done outdoors in the shade of a pole-and-brush shelter.

The Riverine Hohokam usually cremated their dead and placed the ashes in a pottery vessel for burial. The Desert Hohokam disposed of their dead by inhumation, as did most other southwestern prehistoric people. Grave goods were placed with the dead, and much of what we know about Hohokam material culture results from the excavation of burials at Snaketown and other Hohokam sites.

The Hohokam cultivated a variety of crops, including maize (corn), several types of beans, squash, tepary, gourds, and cotton. They also gathered native desert plants for food. Several types of cacti have edible fruits or bulbs, and the Hohokam also utilized beans from the mesquite and roasted agave over open fires. The desert animals that they consumed were deer, javelina, rabbits, bighorn sheep, and small rodents and reptiles. They also ate fish and birds.

The Hohokam apparently conducted considerable trade with other contemporary prehistoric peoples, particularly those to the south in what is now Mexico. Some of the items of Mexican origin found in Hohokam sites are small copper bells, mosaic mirrors, parrot bones, pottery forms, and plant seeds. A few sherds of Mexican pottery were found during the excavations at Snaketown. The large excavated ball courts and rubber balls used in the game are also evidence of contact with prehistoric peoples to the south. The presence of many marine seashells in Hohokam sites indicates trade with people from the Gulf of California or the Pacific coast.

The Hohokam developed some interesting and beautiful arts and crafts. Their typical painted pottery was a red-on-buff type in the form of jars, bowls, plates, scoops, and a few effigy vessels and three-legged shallow bowls. A thick-walled censer was also peculiar to Hohokam potters. Hohokam pottery was constructed by the paddle and anvil method rather than the coiling and scraping technique typical in the prehistoric Southwest. The designs painted on Hohokam pottery were geometric and/or human and animal forms. The pottery is very attractive and exhibits fine artistry and a subtle sense of humor in the painted decoration. No black-on-white or indented corrugated pottery was made in this area.

Stone axes and other ground stone artifacts were usually well made and highly polished. Small stone vessels were polished and carved in relief with animal and human figures. Artifacts peculiar to the Hohokam are small, oblong stone palettes with a raised and sometimes sculptured rim. They have a depressed center that may have been used to mix paint. Some of the most attractive Hohokam artifacts are bracelets, rings, beads, and pendants made of seashells. Some of these are finely carved with figures of frogs, snakes, or birds. Some large shells have etched designs produced by the use of acid obtained from cacti. Small mosaic "mirrors" had one surface covered with pyrite crystals to reflect light.

Less is known of the Desert Hohokam, but their culture seems to have been a less well-developed variation of their Riverine relatives. The people of the Desert branch produced red-on-brown polished pottery rather than the unpolished red-on-buff pottery of the Riverine Hohokam. The arts and crafts of the Desert people had less variety and were generally less well executed. As would be expected, the Desert Hohokam depended more on food gathering and less on irrigation. They were also less influenced by intrusion of the Salado people from the north during the fourteenth century. (The Salado culture is discussed later in this chapter.)

Little remains of the great towns of the Hohokam in the area of present-day Phoenix, Arizona. Few have been carefully excavated, and most have been covered by urban development or leveled for agriculture. Only Casa Grande and Pueblo Grande have been prepared for visitors. The major Hohokam sites are located and described in the section on the Middle Gila and Salt River areas. Some archeologists believe that the modern Pima Indians are descendants of the Riverine Hohokam.

The Mogollon

The Mogollon region is located in southwestern New Mexico and southeastern Arizona. This culture evolved southeast of the Anasazi and east of the Hohokam and was named for the mountains that lie in the New Mexico portion of this area. As with the Anasazi, the Mogollon culture has been divided into branches by archeologists, but much less agreement exists concerning the Mogollon branches and chronology. One theory categorizes the Mogollon into the following six branches.

The earliest Mogollon branch is known as the San Simon. The river for which this branch is named is an intermittent southern tributary of the Gila River in extreme southeastern Arizona. This branch developed as early as 300 B.C. and in its western portion blends into the Hohokam.

The Mimbres branch is situated in the southwestern corner of New Mexico and extends south into northern Chihuahua, Mexico, in the vicinity of the great ruin of Casas Grandes. This branch dates from about 250 B.C. It is noted primarily for the unique, finely made black-on-white pottery that has life forms painted on it.

The Pinelawn branch is located in the upper San Francisco River area of New Mexico and extends slightly into adjacent parts of Arizona. It is an early branch that evolved circa 250 B.C. North of the Mogollon Rim in Arizona at an elevation of about 6,000 feet is the area that was inhabited by the Forestdale branch of the Mogollon. This branch developed about 200 B.C. Several ruins in the White Mountain and Little Colorado areas of this guide are Forestdale villages.

A latter branch of the Mogollon known as the Black River is located between the Salt and Gila rivers in southeastern Arizona. This branch did not evolve until about A.D. 100. Kinishba Ruin is one of the Black River sites included in this guide.

The sixth branch of the Mogollon, known as the Jornada, is in the eastern periphery of the Mogollon region east of the Rio Grande River in south-central New Mexico. This branch is not as well known as some of the others, and only the Three Rivers Site is described in this book.

As with the Anasazi and Hohokam cultures, the Mogollon has been divided into time periods by archeologists who have worked in this area. Again, there is no one accepted sequence. One tentative classification is as follows:

Mogollon 1—300 B.C. to A.D. 400
Mogollon 2—A.D. 400 to 600
Mogollon 3—A.D. 600 to 900
Mogollon 4—A.D. 900 to 1000
Mogollon 5—A.D. 1000 to 1250

Most Mogollones inhabited mountainous areas, but some lived in lower transition zones. Early sites were situated in easily defended locations on the top of a ridge or edge of a mesa. After A.D. 900, most Mogollon villages had moved to the valleys near streams or other water sources.

Early Mogollon dwellings were large round pithouses with storage pits excavated into the floors. The houses within each village were not arranged in any pattern, and the number of houses ranged from a few to more than fifty. In later times, the shape of the pithouses changed to rectangular, and the large houses that may have been used for ceremonial purposes also changed from round to square or rectangular. These structures may be analogous to the kivas of the Anasazi. From A.D. 500 to 1000, the size of

17

Collapsed roof timbers and walls, Kinishba Ruin, Arizona

Mogollon pithouses decreased significantly, while the number of pithouses per village increased. In the Mogollon 4 period, villages became composed of a continuous block of masonry surface rooms that at first were arranged in a single line and later were built in two-story blocks around a plaza.

Although their climate provided more moisture than did that of the Hohokam or Anasazi, the Mogollon seem to have relied less on irrigation than the other two cultures. After A.D. 1000, irrigation among the Mogollon was limited to a few sites such as Grasshopper Ruin in the White Mountains. The Mogollon had a good supply of food animals in most of their area and relied more on hunting than did the desert or plateau dwellers.

Much of what we know about the early Mogollon has been obtained from the dry deposits found in Tularosa Cave. It appears that from A.D. 500 to 700 there was a regression in Mogollon culture with a decrease in amounts of cultivated foods and an increase in gathering. This may have been a local condition that did not extend to other branches.

The first pottery in the Mogollon area, and perhaps the earliest in the entire Southwest, was a plain brown ware known as Alma Plain and Alma Rough and a polished red type named San Francisco Red. Later, a red-on-brown type was added to the brown and red wares. After A.D. 700, Mogollon pottery changed gradually to gray utility and painted black-on-white types, and there was an increase in surface treatments such as indented corrugations. The best-known Mogollon pottery is the black-on-white type made by the people of the Mimbres branch from A.D. 1000 to 1250. Unfortunately, the search for this valuable pottery has resulted in the destruction of most Mimbres sites.

Mogollon burials were of the primary type with the body placed in a flexed or sitting position and buried between or within individual houses.

Food plants of the Mogollon included pinon, mariposa lily, agave, walnuts, acorns, amaranth, tansy mustard, kidney beans, prickly pear, gourds, squash, sunflowers, and corn. They also hunted a variety of food animals, among which were deer, pronghorn antelope, bison, turkey, mountain sheep, rabbits, muskrats, small rodents, birds, and fish.

During Mogollon 4 and 5, there was much intrusion of the Anasazi culture into the Mogollon area. Pottery and architecture were influenced, as shown by the designs on black-on-white pottery and features such as the "T"-shaped doorways at Gila Cliff Dwellings. After A.D. 1000, the Mogollon culture was very similar to that of the Anasazi. In the later part of the Mogollon 5 period, the Anasazi immigration increased the population of the Mogollon area beyond its environmental capacity. This contributed to the abandonment of most of the region by A.D. 1250 to 1300, when the remaining inhabitants moved north to Zuni country.

The architecture of the Mogollon, except for the final period, is poorly preserved and does not lend itself to restoration. Therefore, little remains today. The few exceptions are Gila Cliff Dwellings, Kwilleleykia, and Kinishba, which are described in this guide. The state of New Mexico is restoring a Mimbres site near the Gila River that will be open to the public.

The Salado

In addition to the Anasazi, Mogollon, and Hohokam, other cultures have been named but are less well defined by archeologists. These "minor" cultures encompass smaller areas and populations and often appear to be combinations of two or three of the major cultures where they are contiguous.

One of these cultures is named Salado, which is a Spanish word for "salt." It is not clear where these people came from,

19

although some researchers propose that the Salado originated in the north near the Little Colorado drainage. In any event, by around A.D. 1100 these people were living above the confluence of the Salt and Gila rivers. They also settled to the northwest in the canyons of the northern tributaries of the Salt and to the southeast in the upper Gila River valley.

The typical Salado living structure was a small adobe compound of six to twelve rooms surrounded by a wall. The walls of the rooms were made of unshaped cobbles laid up in adobe or a jacal wall made of vertical sticks plastered with mud. This type of construction does not weather well, and little remains of these sites except rows of cobbles outlining the rooms.

The early Salado made plain red pottery known as Gila Red and black and white ware that has been named Roosevelt Black-on-white, which was made by the Mogollon to the northeast. The Salado had much trade with the Anasazi to the north, as shown by the presence of much pottery from that area.

The Salado, who were mainly hunters and gatherers and who later practiced some agriculture, were primarily mountain dwellers. Much of what we know about the Salado culture has been gained from excavations at the Tonto Ruins near Roosevelt Lake. Artifacts found there include plain red and polychrome pottery, expertly woven cotton cloth, basketry, and fine stone and shell work. The burials at Tonto, as well as at other Salado sites, were inhumations in which the bodies were fully extended. The number of sites and their small size indicate that the Salado population was never very large.

About A.D. 1250, the Salado were making a pottery known as Gila Polychrome, and this is the most diagnostic trait of the Salado culture. Gila Polychrome developed from an earlier type named Pinto Polychrome. The pottery has a red base color, and bowl interiors are entirely slipped in a cream color. Designs are painted on the interior in black, with red sometimes included. This pottery was widely traded to the Hohokam to the south, the Mogollon to the east, and as far south as Casas Grandes in what is now Mexico. Evidence also indicates that it was made outside of the Salado area. Bowls and jars were the most common forms, but ladles, mugs, and effigy vessels were also made.

In the fourteenth century, the Salado had increasing contact with the Riverine Hohokam and Salado influences are evident in Hohokam architecture and crafts. By A.D. 1400, the Salado population was dwindling, and by the middle of the fifteenth century, they had abandoned their homeland in the area of the Tonto Basin. It is probable that the remainder moved south to integrate peacefully with the Hohokam, and some may have moved east into the Mogollon area.

In addition to the Tonto Ruins, other Salado sites included in this guide are: Sierra Ancha, Canyon Creek Ruin, Gila Pueblo, Kinishba, and Besh-ba-gowah. Influences from the Salado culture can be seen at many sites beyond the Salado area, however, including the compound at Casa Grande National Monument.

Dating Prehistoric Sites

Dates of occupation or construction of archeological sites are given when this information is known. Archeologists have developed several techniques to determine the age of a ruin, all of which are somewhat imprecise. Therefore, most of the dates given here should be considered approximations.

One of the more accurate methods of dating prehistoric ruins involves the use of tree rings found in the timbers used to build the structure. Tree-ring width varies each year with the unique weather conditions that influence the yearly growth of the tree. The rings in the timber can be compared to a dated sequence of rings previously collected and can establish the years during which the tree was growing and sometimes the year when it was cut. This is one of the most accurate methods of dating, and a sequence of tree-ring dates for the Southwest has been extended back to the time of Christ. Other dating methods are the Carbon-14 method, the use of dated pottery types, and the archeomagnetic technique.

For the convenience of the reader and the traveler, I have divided the prehistoric Southwest into thirteen geographical areas. These areas are presented in Chapters 2 through 14 of this guide. The areas are visually shown on Maps 3 to 15. These maps show major roads and other features in the areas, but other more detailed maps mentioned above should be consulted for data on secondary roads and other physical features. In each area one or more major towns or cities are recommended as good locations to stay while visiting ruins, museums, and other points of interest in the vicinity. When they are present, locations of campgrounds in the vicinity of the ruins are given. As mentioned in some of the chapters, the seasonal weather conditions should be considered in planning camping and other outdoor activities in the Southwest. Generally

21

this region of the country has excellent weather, but there are often great variations within the region and preplanning can usually assure a safe and comfortable trip. Extended hikes into uninhabited areas of this region should be carefully planned and hikers should be well provisioned because it can be dangerous to venture into this wild and arid country without adequate water, food, clothing, and shelter. Local advice should always be sought when traveling off the main roads or hiking into unfamiliar areas.

I hope that this guide will assist you in having a very safe and enjoyable visit to the prehistoric ruins of the beautiful Southwest.

Northern section of Kuaua Pueblo above the Rio Grande River, Coronado State Monument

Excavations and view tower, Pueblo Grande, Phoenix, Arizona

Sinagua masonry walls built on rocks, Wupatki Pueblo, Arizona

Map 3
Prehistoric Ruins of the Northern Rio Grande

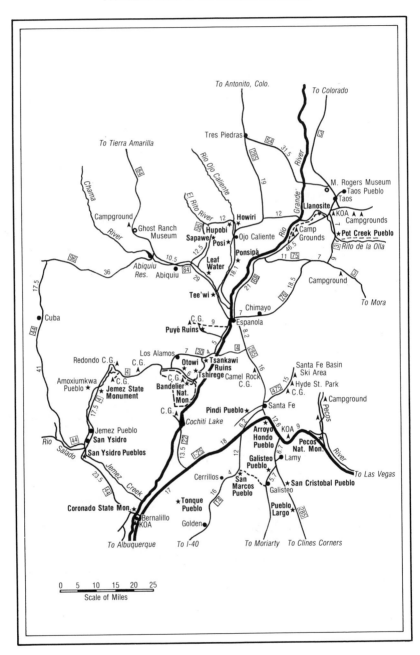

To Antonito, Colo.

To Colorado

To Tierra Amarilla

Tres Piedras

M. Rogers Museum
Taos Pueblo
Taos

Llanosite

KOA
Campgrounds

Howiri

Camp Grounds

Pot Creek Pueblo

Ghost Ranch Museum

Hupobi
Sapawe
Posi
Ojo Caliente

Rito de la Olla

Campground

Ponsipá

Leaf Water

Abiquiu Res. Abiquiu

Tee'wi

Chimayo

To Mora

Cuba

C.G.

Espanola

Puyé Ruins

Los Alamos

Otowi
Tsankawi Ruins
Tshirege

Santa Fe Basin
Ski Area

Redondo C.G.
C.G.

Camel Rock C.G.

Hyde St. Park
C.G.

Amoxiumkwa Pueblo

C.G.

Bandelier Nat. Mon.

Campground

Jemez State Monument

C.G.

Pindi Pueblo

Santa Fe

Cochiti Lake

Jemez Pueblo
San Ysidro
San Ysidro Pueblos

Arroyo Hondo Pueblo

KOA

Pecos Nat. Mon.

Galisteo Pueblo

Lamy

To Las Vegas

Cerrillos

San Marcos Pueblo

Galisteo

San Cristobal Pueblo

Coronado State Mon.

Tonque Pueblo

Pueblo Largo

Bernalillo
KOA

Golden

To Albuquerque

To I-40

To Moriarty   To Clines Corners

0   5   10   15   20   25
Scale of Miles

II

Northern Rio Grande Area

This area contains many significant prehistoric ruins, and some of the descendants of the inhabitants of these sites now live in contemporary pueblos along the Rio Grande River and at Zuni and Hopi. Museums and other research institutions have carried on excavations and other studies since the latter years of the nineteenth century. Persons interested in prehistory or history of the Southwest will find much to see in this area. All of the sites in this section are of the Rio Grande branch of the Anasazi culture.

For purposes of this guide, the Northern Rio Grande is roughly bounded by Taos, New Mexico, on the north and Bernalillo on the south. It extends east to the Pecos River and west to Jemez Creek. Santa Fe is a good central location from which to visit the ruins in the Northern Rio Grande. Camping is not available in Santa Fe, but the Camel Rock Campground is nine miles north of town on Interstate-25, and Hyde Park State Park is twelve miles to the northeast. Camel Rock Campground is on land owned by the Tesuque Pueblo and can accommodate pickup campers, trailers, or tents.

Santa Fe has many stores selling Indian arts and crafts, some of which have exceptionally high-quality merchandise. There are also a number of good art galleries in Santa Fe, and in the summer the famous Santa Fe Opera presents its programs. In the winter months there is skiing nearby.

Santa Fe is fortunate to have several outstanding museums containing collections of the material culture of the prehistoric Southwest. Two are located in the Camino Lejo museum complex just off the Old Santa Fe Trail. These are the Laboratory of Anthropology and the Wheelwright Museum (formerly the Museum of Navajo Ceremonial Art). The Governor's Palace Museum is located on the north side of the plaza and includes a gift shop with a good selection of Indian arts and books. The Fine Arts Museum is just off the northwest corner of the plaza. One of the best opportunities to buy Indian arts directly from the artists is the annual Santa Fe Indian market held in August. The entire plaza is filled with booths containing examples of the finest work of contemporary Indian artists.

Santa Fe is one of the few truly unique towns in the United States. Its architecture and culture make it a "must" for any one interested in the Southwest. The prize-winning novel *Lamy of Santa Fe* by Paul Horgan is recommended reading for those interested in the Spanish period of this region. A broader history of the area is the two-volume work, *Great River: The Rio Grande,* also by Horgan.

Travelers to Santa Fe can spend a day or as much as a week visiting the prehistoric sites in this area. To the north are the sites near Taos and the Valley of the Chama River. Bandelier National Monument has some of the best preserved and restored ruins in the area, and Puye' Ruins on the nearby Santa Clara Indian Reservation are definitely worth a trip. Good camping and some fishing are available in Santa Clara Canyon near Puye'. Southwest of Santa Fe are the pueblo ruins near Jemez. The Pecos Ruin National Monument southeast of Santa Fe over scenic Glorieta Pass is the farthest west of all the major pueblo sites. South of Santa Fe are the several major pueblos of the Galisteo Valley. If time is limited, Bandelier, Puye', and Pecos are the three restored ruins that are easily accessible.

The following section presents more information on the location, characteristics, age, and archeological work that has been done at the major prehistoric ruins of the Northern Rio Grande. The locations of most of the major ruins in this area are shown on Map #3.

Pot Creek Pueblo (LA 260). This pueblo ruin is located in Taos County near the confluence of the Rito de la Olla, locally known as Pot Creek, and the Rio Grande de Ranchos. The site is about nine miles southeast of the town of Taos. The ruin is located across the road from the Fort Burgwin Research Center. Personnel from Fort Burgwin, which is operated by Southern Methodist University, excavated at Pot Creek from 1957 to 1967. Some artifacts from the pueblo are housed in the research center. This ruin is on private land, and permission to visit it should be obtained at the research center.

Pot Creek is a nine-mound complex with mounds ranging in size from 25 feet in diameter to 30 by 150 feet. Several kiva and pithouse depressions are distributed among the mounds, and the complex is surrounded by a pine-juniper forest. Parts of three mounds and one kiva have been excavated. Pot Creek Pueblo was inhabited from about A.D. 1000 to 1350.

Llano Site (LA 1892) is west of Pot Creek Pueblo on the south side of the Rio Grande de Ranchos near its confluence with the Rio Taos. No walls are standing, but some depressions and a sherd area are visible. This site consisted of two small pueblo units about 100 yards apart. One pueblo had seven rooms, and the larger had seventeen rooms and a subterranean, circular kiva nineteen feet in diameter. The tree-ring dates for this site are A.D. 1207 to 1239. Llano Site was excavated by Jean A. Jeancon in 1920.

In the valley of the Chama River, the major western tributary of the Rio Grande, there are a number of large pueblo sites. All of these sites are in Rio Arriba County, New Mexico.

Leaf Water Site (LA 300) is located fifteen miles west of Espanola, New Mexico. It is a large, quadrangular pueblo about sixty-five by ninety yards in size. Rooms were situated on the north,east, and west sides of the pueblo surrounding a plaza and two kivas. The pueblo was constructed of coursed adobe and sandstone. Two pithouses underlie the more recent structure. The pueblo was built in about A.D. 1250. Stanley Stubbs excavated part of this site in 1953.

Te-ewi Pueblo (LA 252) is on the west bank of the Chama River near its junction with the Rio Oso. It was a large, rectangular pueblo, part of which was two stories in height. Two plazas and eleven kivas were found. Originally, ten stone shrines were placed around the pueblo near the edge of the mesa. Te-ewi was occupied from A.D. 1250 to 1550. From 1950 to 1951, Stanley Stubbs excavated twenty-seven rooms, four kivas, and ten shrines. Llano, Leaf Water, and Te-ewi are on private property.

The Ojo Caliente River, a northern tributary of the Chama, has several large pueblo ruins along its valley. Going upstream, the five major ruins are named **Ponsipa'akwaye, Nute, Posi** (LA 632),

Hupobi (LA 380), and **Howiri** (LA 71). Posi is across the river from the town of Ojo Caliente, and Hupobi and Howiri are a few miles north. Howiri dates from the Pueblo IV period, A.D. 1300 to 1700; part of it was excavated by the Laboratory of Anthropology in 1979. These sites all contain Biscuitware pottery, indicating that they date from circa A.D. 1375 to 1500. Biscuitware is a black-on-gray type named for its resemblance to the biscuit stage in the production of porcelain china. These ruins are characterized by their large size, open quadrangular shape, adobe and boulder walls, and large numbers of kivas. Little professional excavation has been done in these ruins, and they have been pothunted for many years; therefore, little of value remains.

Eight miles up the El Rito River, another northern tributary of the Chama, is the huge ruin known as **Sapawe'** (LA 306). This ruin, on the west bank of the river, is nearly 200 yards across the main section. It was built of adobe and has a large central kiva and more than twenty other kivas. This is also a Biscuitware site. Little has been published concerning the excavation of Sapawe'.

A major ruin near Santa Fe is **Pindi Pueblo** (LA 1), excavated from 1932 to 1933 by Stanley Stubbs and later by amateurs. It was left open after the private excavation, and most of it has been washed away by rain. Pindi was located six miles west of Santa Fe on the north bank of the Santa Fe River. It was occupied from A.D. 1050 to 1349 and consisted of a large pueblo of adobe construction with five kivas.

Pecos National Monument* is actually located in the Pecos River drainage, but because of its proximity to the Rio Grande ruins, it is included in this section. Pecos is one of the best excavated and restored sites in this area. It is located in San Miguel County twenty-five miles southeast of Santa Fe on Interstate 25. It is situated on the east side of Pecos Arroyo, three miles south of the town of Pecos, New Mexico. Directional signs from Interstate 25 make it easy to find. North of Pecos Monument is the Pecos Wilderness Area, which enables the traveler to combine a visit to Pecos National Monument with some hiking or backpacking.

Pecos consists of ruins of two pueblos and a Spanish mission church. The main ruin, known as **Pecos Pueblo** (LA 625), is a very large, multistoried pueblo with at least 660 rooms and 22 kivas constructed around an open plaza. Pecos may have housed as many as 2,000 inhabitants. The pueblo was built around A.D. 1450 and occupied until 1838, when the remaining seventeen inhabitants left to join their Towa tribesmen at Jemez Pueblo. The large Spanish church was built in the 1620s. This church was 170 feet long, 90 feet wide at the transept, and 39 feet wide inside the nave. Some of the nave walls were nine feet thick.

A self-guided trail leads to the convento, church, remains of two pueblo ruins, and an interesting restored kiva. Much of the trail can be used by persons in wheelchairs, and the restrooms are accessible.

A second ruin named **Forked Lightning** (LA 672) is one mile southwest of Pecos Pueblo. It is part of Pecos National Monument, but permission is necessary to visit it. It is an earlier site and was occupied from A.D. 1225 to 1300. Other pueblos contemporary with Forked Lightning in this vicinity are: **Arrowhead Ruin** (LA 251), to the northwest toward Glorieta; **Loma Lathrop Ruin** (LA 277), a short distance northeast of Pecos; and **Dick's Ruin** (LA 276) and **Rowe Ruin** (LA 108), in the Pecos River valley to the southeast. It is probable that the inhabitants of Forked Lightning and some of the other earlier sites built Pecos Pueblo in a more easily defended location to protect themselves against the attacks of the Apaches to the east.

Pecos Pueblo was excavaged by Alfred Kidder in the years 1915 to 1929. His report published in 1936 is a classic report of archeological research and still makes fascinating reading (Kidder and Shepard, 1936). Camping is not available at the monument, but a good KOA campground is located near Glorieta a few miles east of Pecos, and wilderness camping is available to the north.

Another major site, **Arroyo Hondo Pueblo** (LA 12), is located on the south rim of Arroyo Hondo, four and one-half miles south of the plaza in Santa Fe. This was an 1,100-room adobe pueblo structure. The site consists of twenty-four room blocks and ten plazas and covered six acres. The pueblo contained many turkey pens, indicating a major domestication of this native bird.

This site was first occupied around A.D. 1300, when a few families built one or two small room blocks. The population grew rapidly and by A.D. 1335 had reached its peak of an estimated 2,000 persons. The population then declined, and by the mid four-teenth century, the pueblo was abandoned or retained only a very small occupancy. In the 1370s, Arroyo Hondo Pueblo was reoccupied, and the new inhabitants rebuilt nine room blocks and three plazas. A second decline in population resulted in permanent abandonment circa A.D. 1425.

This site was carefully studied and excavated by the School of American Research under the direction of Douglas Schwartz from

1971 to 1974. The site is located on private property, and the excavations have been backfilled, leaving little to be seen.

A little more than one mile east (upstream) of Arroyo Hondo Pueblo, in Arroyo Hondo, is **Upper Arroyo Hondo Pueblo** (LA 76). This adobe pueblo had forty-five to fifty rooms. The site is on a low hill above a spring in the arroyo. It was occupied from about A.D. 1287 to 1316 and is also on private land.

Several large pueblo ruins are located in the Galisteo Valley south of Santa Fe. Some of these ruins were still occupied into historic times. Four of these ruins are **Galisteo Pueblo, Pueblo Largo** (LA 183), **San Cristobal Pueblo** (LA 80), and **San Marcos Pueblo** (LA 98). Nels Nelson excavated some of these ruins from 1912 to 1914. He was one of the first American archeologists to use stratigraphy to determine the chronological development of sites.

Galisteo Pueblo (LA 309) is above the present town of Galisteo on the banks of Arroyo Galisteo. It is a medium-size pueblo of adobe that lacks uniformity. Galisteo had a combined prehistoric and historic total of 1,640 rooms. There are four large refuse heaps. Nelson excavated twenty-five rooms from 1912 to 1914.

Pueblo Largo (LA 183) is located on the Canada Estacada, approximately thirty miles south of Santa Fe. It is south of San Cristobal on the western edge of the escarpment. In spite of its name, it is the smallest of the Galisteo pueblos, containing 489 ground-floor rooms in six house blocks and evidence of one kiva. A shrine is located 600 feet to the southeast on the edge of a flat-topped hill. Nelson excavated only four rooms here and estimated that Building Number 4 dated to the early 1400s.

San Cristobal Pueblo (LA 80) is eight miles southeast of Lamy, New Mexico, and six miles east of Galisteo on the banks of the Arroyo San Cristobal. It is a large pueblo divided into 19 to 20 house units with a total of 1,645 ground-floor rooms. At least four kivas and eight refuse heaps were found. The site is 1,300 feet by 2,000 feet in size. Nels Nelson excavated 239 rooms and one kiva at San Cristobal. It is not known when this pueblo was built, but it was abandoned between A.D. 1680 and 1692 during the Pueblo Rebellion. Some interesting petroglyphs are located on cliffs near this ruin.

San Marcos Pueblo (LA 98) is eighteen miles south of Santa Fe on the north side of Arroyo San Marcos, a tributary of the Rio Galisteo. As is true of most of the ruins in the Galisteo Valley, San Marcos is located on private property, and permission should be obtained to visit it. In 1980, a residence was being built over part of this ruin.

San Marcos is a large ruin consisting of a number of low but distinct mounds representing house blocks. One very large building had eight wings. Walls and floors were constructed of coursed adobe. There is also the ruin of a seventeenth-century Spanish mission. This ruin was excavated in 1915 by Nels Nelson, and later one room was excavated by Erik Reed. The dates of occupancy are estimated at A.D. 1350 to 1680.

An interesting finding at several of the Galisteo ruins was a type of black-on-white pottery very similar to Mesa Verde Black-on-White, which was made north of the San Juan River in southwestern Colorado.

Other ruins in the Galisteo Valley have been named: **Pueblo Colorado** (881 rooms), **Pueblo She'** (1,543 rooms), **Pueblo Blanco** (1,450 rooms), and **Pueblo San Lazaro** (1,940 rooms). The Galisteo ruins are quite similar, and none have been restored. Some pictographs may be seen on the vertical cliff above Pueblo Colorado and on the escarpment north of Pueblo Blanco. All of these ruins are on private land, and some landowners will not give permission to enter their property.

Bandelier National Monument*. This is the place to go if you have limited time to see the ruins in the Northern Rio Grande. It has the greatest variety of sites and terrain and probably appeals to a wider range of ages and interests than any other single area.

This national monument was dedicated in 1916 and is named for Adolph F. A. Bandelier, the pioneer Swiss-American archeologist. Bandelier wrote an ethnohistorical novel, *The Delight-makers,* in 1890 based on his perceptions of the prehistoric dwellers of Frijoles Canyon. This is a fascinating story and is highly recommended to those visiting Bandelier. It brings a human element to the ancient ruins and makes them more meaningful.

Bandelier National Monument is in Sandoval County, New Mexico, forty-six miles northwest of Santa Fe. To reach it, travel north on Interstate 25 to the town of Pojoaque, then turn west on New Mexico No. 4 to the monument entrance. It occupies part of the Pajarito Plateau. The monument is forty-six square miles in area, most of which is wilderness, providing a good opportunity for hiking in the backcountry. The most accessible features are in Frijoles Canyon near the visitors' center. These include **Tyuonyi Pueblo, Long House,** a talus ruin, **Ceremonial Cave,** and **Rainbow**

House (LA 217) one-half mile down the canyon from the visitors' center.

Tyuonyi (LA 82) is the most impressive ruin and has been excavated and well stabilized. It is a masonry pueblo of 250 ground-floor rooms and three kivas. The pueblo is generally circular in shape, and parts of it were two or three stories in height. There was a single narrow entrance to the pueblo, indicating that the pueblo may have been designed for defensive purposes.

Visitors may take a self-guided one-mile Ruins Trail that leads from the visitors' center through Tyuonyi and up to the Ceremonial Cave, 150 feet above the stream. To get into the cave, you must climb two ladders, totaling 100 feet. This is fun for children, who may find this the best part of the trip. The cave contains a small restored kiva and was used from about A.D. 1250 to 1600.

The trail beyond Tyuonyi leads along the base of the cliff past Talus House, Long House, petroglyphs, and on to Ceremonial Cave. This trail is easy talking, and persons in wheelchairs or the disabled can reach Tyuonyi. For those with more energy and time, a trail leads across the stream and up the southern canyon wall to **Frijolito Ruin** (LA 78), an excavated site. Frijolito is not accessible to disabled persons.

A variety of other trails taking from two hours to two days to hike lead to the backcountry ruins of **Yapashi**, the **Stone Lions**, **Painted Cave, San Miguel**, and many smaller unnamed sites. Painted Cave is located in Capulin Canyon. It is about thirty feet above the canyon floor and, although the cave is no longer accessible, the painted designs can be clearly seen from below. Detailed information can be obtained at the visitors' center concerning the trails. The book titled *A Hiker's Guide to Bandelier National Monument* by Dorothy Hoard is the written source of information on the backcountry trails.

The visitors' center has a small museum with an interpretive program. Bandelier National Monument is open year-round, but the small lodge and lunchrooms are open in the summer only. The address of Frijoles Canyon Lodge is Los Alamos, New Mexico 87544, telephone (505) 672-3961. A national park service campground with drinking water, fireplaces, and restrooms is on the mesa above Frijoles Canyon.

The first scientific excavations done in Bandelier were carried out by Edgar L. Hewett from 1908 to 1910, and since then, studies have been done at Rainbow House and small sites endangered by the construction of Cochiti Reservoir. The tree-ring dates from

Tyuonyi range from A.D. 1383 to 1466.

Tsankawi Ruins* are in a separate section of Bandelier Monument located about one mile from the monument entrance off New Mexico Route No. 4. A sign marks the parking area, and pamphlets are available as trail guides to points of interest. Tsankawi is situated on top of a mesa that has a beautiful view. The site is rectangular in shape, enclosing a large plaza. The ruin is unexcavated and consisted of about 250 rooms, part of which were three stories high. A one-half-mile foot trail leads to the mesa top and back along the cliff to some petroglyphs. Part of the trail is deeply worn into the soft tuff. The site also includes ten kivas and burial areas outside the open corners of the pueblo. Tsankawi was occupied by circa A.D. 1400 to 1600. Edgar Hewett excavated part of this ruin in 1908, but the excavations were backfilled, and no restoration has been done. Tsankawi Ruin itself is not of great interest to most persons, but the view, trail, and petroglyphs make a visit to it worthwhile.

Otowi Ruins (Potsuwi'i) (LA 169) is northwest of Tsankawi, about five miles west of the point where the Rio Grande River enters White Rock Canyon.

The main pueblo is a cluster of five room blocks, four of which are connected by a wall. The room blocks were terraced into two to four stories and contained 450 ground-floor rooms. There was an estimated total of 700 rooms and 10 circular kivas. Cave dwellings are common along the nearby cliffs. These dwellings are composed of rows of masonry rooms in front of rear rooms dug into the soft tuff by the prehistoric inhabitants. Some of them are called "tent rocks" because of their conical shape. Two trash mounds from which 150 burials were excavated are located south of the pueblo. Otowi was inhabited from about A.D. 1100 to 1600, and some of the former inhabitants moved to San Ildefonso Pueblo. Edgar Hewett excavated here in 1905, and L. L. W. Wilson continued the work in 1906 to 1907. Camping is available in Santa Clara Canyon. Otowi is on Department of Energy land, and visitors are not encouraged.

Another very large site on the Pajarito Plateau is **Tshirege Ruin** (LA 170) in Sandoval County. This ruin is six miles west of the Rio Grande River on Tshirege Mesa and is situated on the north side of Pajarito Canyon one mile west of White Rock housing area. It is a very large "U"-shaped pueblo of four stories built of blocks of pumice and tuff. It had more than 600 ground-floor rooms and an estimated total of 1,500 rooms and 10 circular kivas. A cliff village extended for three-fourths of a mile along the cliff below the mesa. Some good petroglyphs can be seen on the cliff face below the pueblo. This site was excavated by Edgar Hewett in the early 1900s.

Puye' Cliff Dwellings* (LA 47) are in southern Rio Arriba County on the Santa Clara Indian Reservation. They are situated on a mesa top and on the talus slope below.

Puye' consists of a large masonry, mesa-top pueblo or community house and numerous talus units. Ten circular kiva depressions are present in and outside the pueblo. The talus units extend for more than one mile along the cliff. A prehistoric reservoir is situated 120 feet west of the pueblo.

Talus units on cliff face, Puye' Ruins, Santa Clara Indian Reservation

Puye' was occupied from A.D. 1530 to 1560, and the inhabitants may have been the ancestors of the present Santa Clara Indians, who hold an annual celebration here in late July. This celebration consists of dancing and other festivities on the mesa top.

This site was excavated by Edgar Hewett in 1907 to 1909. The ruin is owned by the Santa Clarans, who operate nearby campgrounds in Santa Clara Canyon and charge a fee of one dollar per

Restored talus unit with protruding roof beams, Puyé Ruins, New Mexico

Restored mesa top pueblo, Puyé Ruins

person to see the ruins. A trail leads up the cliff past the talus units to the mesa top, or you may drive to the top of the mesa to see the pueblo. There are good campsites in the canyon and some fishing in several ponds and the stream. Small fees are charged for camping and fishing.

Coronado State Monument, the site of **Kuaua Pueblo*** (LA 187), is five miles west of Interstate 25 on Highway No. 44, through Bernalillo, New Mexico, to the entrance on the west bank of the Rio Grande River. Kuaua Pueblo had about 1,200 ground-floor rooms and additional rooms in several upper stories in some portions. It was built of adobe in a large rectangular shape with a central plaza. This site was thoroughly excavated and is a good example of a sixteenth-century pueblo. The outstanding feature of Kuaua is the restored painted kiva in the plaza. The fine polychrome murals have been restored and are the best example of this art form in the Rio Grande.

Excavated adobe rooms at Kuaua Pueblo, Coronado State Monument, New Mexico

Puaray Pueblo (LA 716), formerly a detached section of Coronado State Monument, is located approximately two to three miles south of Kuaua on a bluff above the Rio Grande. It has been destroyed, and all that remains is a sherd area in a gravel pit.

Visitors to Coronado may take a walking tour through the ruin, enter the painted kiva, and see the artifacts in the visitors' center. The monument is open 9:00 AM to 5:00 PM during the summer months and 9:00 AM to 5:00 PM Tuesday through Saturday in the winter. Holiday hours are 2:00 PM to 5:00 PM. Most of the monument is accessible to persons in wheelchairs.

The pueblo was excavated by Edgar Hewett in 1934 to 1939. The dates of occupation were A.D. 1300 to prior to 1680. Camping is available at a state park adjacent to the monument and at KOA in Bernalillo. There is a good Indian arts store in Bernalillo owned and operated by James Silva.

Up Jemez Canyon from Bernalillo are several ruins in the vicinity of Jemez, two of which are Guisewa, at Jemez State Monument, and nearby Amoxiumkwa.

Jemez State Monument* is in Jemez Canyon sixteen miles north on Highway No. 4 from its junction with Highway No. 44. It is at the northern edge of the town of Jemez Springs. This state monument consists of the ruins of a pueblo and a seventeenth-century Spanish mission church. The pueblo, known as **Guisewa***(LA 679), was inhabited from prior to A.D. 1300 to 1696. It is built of sandstone and adobe in the shape of two hollow rectangles at least two stories high. At the peak of its population, it housed about 800 persons. Three circular kivas have been excavated at Guisewa, and others probably exist in the unexcavated portions. The pueblo extends under the highway and under the present monastery on the opposite side.

Excavations at Jemez State Monument were first carried out by Frederick W. Hodge in 1910; in 1921 to 1922, Edgar Hewett did more extensive work; and in 1935 to 1937, Civilian Conservation Corps (CCC) personnel did more excavation and stabilization. The visitors' center was built in 1965. There is a short self-guided interpretive trail leading through the ruins of the church and pueblo. The monument is open to visitors from 9:00 AM to 5:00 PM Wednesday through Sunday, and 2:00 to 5:00 PM on holidays. Most of this monument is accessible to disabled persons.

Nearby Jemez Springs is a good place to stop and picnic and take a swim. This is particularly fun for the children. Several small public campgrounds are located in the vicinity, including Redondo

Campground, 11.3 miles northeast of Jemez Springs on Highway No. 4.

Amoxiumkwa Pueblo (LA 481) is west and above Jemez Springs. It is a large masonry ruin, 200 by 350 yards in size. There are seven kiva depressions, one of which is larger than the others. Nearby is a reservoir depression 150 feet in diameter. Little professional excavation has been done at Amoxiumkwa, and therefore little is known about it. There were both prehistoric and historic occupations. The pueblo's inhabitants probably moved to Giusewa or Jemez Pueblo when the Spanish concentrated the population of the area at these two locations.

South of both Jemez and the town of San Ysidro are the **San Ysidro Pueblos** (FB 115, FB 142). This site consisted of two adobe pueblos that were one-story in height and about 500 meters apart. In 1962 to 1963 Franklin Barnett excavated thirty-three rooms in these two pueblos. The sites are on private land and have been badly "pothunted" over the years. Based on the pottery found, the dates for the pueblos are A.D. 1350 to 1490.

Tonque Pueblo (LA 240) is an important pueblo in Sandoval County north of Albuquerque. It is one mile east of the San Felipe Pueblo boundary and is situated in a saucerlike depression in Tonque Arroyo. Tonque covers a total area of thirty-eight acres and consists of three nearly parallel house blocks with plazas in between. There were a total of 1,500 rooms and a great kiva fifty feet in diameter. Several excavations have been done at Tonque, including 218 rooms excavated by Nels Nelson in 1914, 50 rooms excavated by Richard Bice, and 94 rooms excavated by Franklin Barnett in 1962 to 1964. Tonque was a center of production of glaze ware pottery during the Pueblo IV period. Pottery from this pueblo was widely traded to other pueblos in the Northern Rio Grande. The excavations have been backfilled and little remains to be seen.

Ruins of La Purisima Concepcion a 17th century Spanish church at Quarai State Monument

Masonry pueblo walls, Abo State Monument, New Mexico

Map 4

Prehistoric Ruins of the Middle Rio Grande

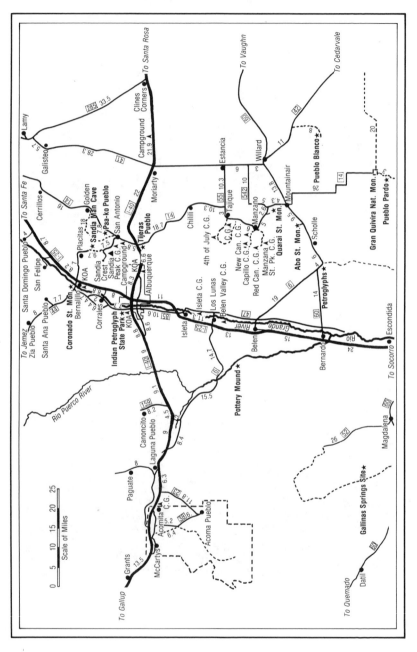

III

Middle Rio Grande Area

This area was less densely inhabited in prehistoric times than the wetter northern part of the Rio Grande; therefore, fewer large sites are located here. The Middle Rio Grande area extends from Albuquerque, New Mexico, on the north to the Tularosa Basin, north of Alamogordo, in the southeast. Magdalena, New Mexico, marks the western edge of the area, and Chupadero Mesa and the Manzano Mountains are the eastern boundary. The region contains a variety of topographical features and small towns in the valley of the Rio Grande. To the east is a large area of mountains and mesas. The locations of the prehistoric sites described in this chapter are shown on Map #4, except for Three Rivers Ruin which is on Map #5. All of the sites in this chapter are Rio Grande Anasazi except Three Rivers, which is Mogollon.

In the northern portion is Albuquerque, the major city in New Mexico and a good place to stay while visiting sites. There are abundant lodging facilities and restaurants in this interesting city. Good campgrounds are located at Spear Cross Ranch to the east in Tijeras Canyon and at Riverside Park to the west on Interstate 40. A number of good restaurants are located in Albuquerque, many specializing in Mexican dishes and excellent beef. The historic Old Town section of Albuquerque has many stores selling Indian arts and crafts. As in other towns, it is best to buy only from reputable, established dealers who will stand behind their merchandise.

One place that persons studying Southwest prehistory should not miss is the Maxwell Museum of Anthropology at the University of New Mexico, University Street and Roma Avenue NE. This museum has fine exhibits and excellent research collections for the scholar. It is open from 9:00 AM to 4:00 PM, Monday through Friday. Another good museum is the Museum of Albuquerque, located at 2000 Mountain Road, NW, Old Town, Albuquerque.

Paa-ko Pueblo (LA 162) is located in the Sandia Mountains twenty-five miles northeast of Albuquerque and one mile north of San Antonio. Two major sections, north and south, comprise this Anasazi masonry and adobe pueblo. Both sections were occupied during prehistoric times, but only the southwest portion was occupied in historic times. The buildings are multistoried blocks of rooms surrounding plazas that contain kivas. Paa-ko was occupied from A.D. 1350 to 1550 and was excavated by Marjorie F. Lambert in 1935 to 1937.

Ten miles southwest of Paa-ko in Tijeras Canyon, near the junction of Interstate 40 and New Mexico Highway Number 14 is **Tijeras Pueblo** (LA 581). This site was under excavation by personnel of the University of New Mexico from 1971 to 1976. James Judge directed this work from 1971 to 1973 and the work was under the supervision of Linda Cordell from 1974 to 1976.

Tijeras Pueblo was built in A.D. 1300 and was occupied until A.D. 1425. The original structure had 200 rooms of adobe and jacal construction, and a few masonry rooms. The rooms were built in houseblocks arranged in a circle with an opening to the north. A large round kiva built of a double course of stone blocks was situated in the center of the community. Research indicates that during the late 1300s the pueblo was partially abandoned, and a new smaller pueblo was built over the southern section. This new structure of about 100 rooms was built in the form of a "U", open to the east. The old circular kiva was abandoned, and a new rectangular one was constructed in the western end of the pueblo facing the plaza.

Tijeras Pueblo was permanently abandoned about A.D. 1425, and it now consists of a mound of backfilled excavation marked by a sign near the road.

Northeast of Albuquerque in scenic Las Huertas Canyon is the well-known site named **Sandia Cave***. It is located six miles up the canyon from the small village of Placitas, New Mexico, on Road No. 44. This section of No. 44 is a narrow, winding gravel road. From Albuquerque, the best route is to go east on Interstate 25 to

Tijeras, then north on New Mexico No. 14 to No. 44, the road up Sandia Peak. There is less gravel on this route, and it is a beautiful drive. From a small marked parking lot, a one-half-mile trail ascends the canyon wall to the cave mouth below the rim. A picnic ground is located along the trail. Sandia Cave is situated high on the vertical canyon wall in a seemingly inaccessible position. The site has not been restored, but it is worth the short hike, and there is a scenic view down the canyon and across the Rio Grande to the distant Jemez Mountains.

Sandia Cave may have been occupied as early as 25,000 years ago, although this early date has recently been questioned. In any event, it is the only early man site prepared for visitation in the Southwest. The most recent occupation of the cave was in Pueblo III times. This site is best known for the ancient Sandia points named for the cave. Sandia Cave, excavated by Frank C. Hibben in 1940, is a long, narrow cave approximately 300 feet long and only 30 feet wide.

On the west mesa of Albuquerque is **Indian Petroglyph State Park***. It can be reached by going north from Interstate 40 at the Coors Road exit, then angling left on Atrisco Drive for two and one-half miles to a directional sign. A trail leads up the cliff past a number of petroglyphs to the top of West Mesa. These petroglyphs are prehistoric figures pecked into the surface of boulders or the cliff face. The figures include human and animal forms and a variety of geometric figures. The meaning and age of these petroglyphs is unknown, but some of the figures are still used today by the Pueblo Indians of the Northern Rio Grande.

Indian Petroglyph State Park was created through the efforts of Col. and Mrs. Jim Bain and other members of the Albuquerque Archeological Society. The Bains and Ruth Armstrong spent more than one year photographing and recording the many petroglyphs in the area of the present park. In 1968, the Bains were able to persuade one of the landowners to deed his land to the state of New Mexico for a park. This park is a good choice for persons who want to see prehistoric rock art and who want to take a short hike over the volcanic terrain of the Southwest.

The major ruins south of Albuquerque are located to the east of the Rio Grande on the eastern slope of the Manzano Mountains. These ruins include: Quarai State Monument, Abo State Monument, Gran Quivira National Monument, and Pueblo Pardo. These are the remains of four of the eleven pueblos that were occupied at the time of the Spanish entrada. Part of this area was named the Salinas Province by the Spanish because of the natural salt ponds in the vicinity. Other major pueblos were named **Chilili, Tabirá, Tajique, Cuarac,** and **Senecu.**

Quarai State Monument* (LA 95) is in Torrance County, New Mexico, ten miles north of Mountainair via Highway #10. The ruins are situated in a valley on the eastern slope of the Manzano Mountains.

The site consists of the ruins of a large seventeenth-century Spanish church and its convento in addition to a large, partially excavated pueblo ruin. The inhabitants of the pueblo were Tiwa-speaking people whose culture combined Anasazi and Mogollon cultural traits. Quarai was inhabited from A.D. 1300 to 1672. Excavations at Quarai were carried out in 1913, 1920, and 1934 to 1935, and in 1939 to 1940, Joseph H. Toulouse did excavation and stabilization. The monument has a visitors' center, where exhibits illustrate the life of the inhabitants and display artifacts found during the digs. A self-guided trail interprets the history of the site.

Campgrounds are located at Manzano State Park and in Cibola National Forest southwest of Torreon, New Mexico.

Ten miles southwest of Mountainair on U.S. No. 60 is **Abo State Monument*** (LA 97). Abo, like Quarai, is the ruin of a seventeenth-century Spanish church and the pueblo it served. The church was one of the finest in early New Mexico. The large unexcavated pueblo was inhabited about A.D. 1300 by people who spoke the now extinct Piro language. The pueblo is built of sandstone masonry and includes a kiva that was later part of the wall of the Catholic Church complex. Excavations in 1938 to 1939 by Joseph H. Toulouse revealed, in addition to the church, a convento, courts, a kiva, "turkey pens," and corrals. Abo was inhabited from about A.D. 1300 to 1672, when raiding Apaches burned the church and killed the priest. The survivors probably moved to other pueblos in the vicinity.

No services or visitors' facilities are available at Abo, but campgrounds are located nearby in Cibola National Forest.

Gran Quivira National Monument* is twenty-six miles southeast of Mountainair on New Mexico No. 14. It is situated on an east-west ridge of Chupadero Mesa.

The monument is composed of the ruins of **Pueblo de las Humanas** (LA 120) and two seventeenth-century Spanish churches. The first church was built in A.D. 1629. By A.D. 1600, this pueblo was the largest in the region. It was inhabited by people speaking the Piro language. Their cultural characteristics indicate that they

San Gregorio de Abo Mission, Abo State Monument, New Mexico

Massive masonry walls of Spanish church at Abo State Monument, New Mexico

45

may have come from the west, where they may have been related to the ancestors of the Zunis and Hopis. Twenty-one house mounds covered a group of single and multistoried buildings constructed of gray-blue limestone and mud mortar. The burials found here were unusual for this area in that two-thirds of them were cremations, and no grave goods were found with them. Alden Hayes excavated 226 rooms, 6 kivas, 5 cisterns, and a number of refuse dumps at this site. It was determined that this was the last pueblo in the area to produce black-on-white pottery. Pueblo de las Humanas was occupied from circa A.D. 1300 to 1675.

The monument is open 8:00 AM to 5:00 PM daily, year-round. The superintendent's address is Route 1, Mountainair, New Mexico 87036. A visitors' center with exhibits is open to the public, as well as a trail through the ruins that takes about twenty minutes to hike. The monument has a picnic ground but no camping facilities. The visitors' center is accessible to persons in wheelchairs as is the trail to the ruins, although it is rather steep in two places.

It is recommended that all three of the sites mentioned above be visited in one full day by persons staying in the vicinity. The close proximity, easy accessibility, and cultural relationships of Abo, Quarai, and Gran Quivira make them a good unit for a single visit.

Three miles south of Gran Quivira in the east-central part of the Gran Quivira quadrangle, on the east end of a low ridge, is **Pueblo Pardo** (LA 83).

Pueblo Pardo consists of a cluster of nearly adjoining masonry room units and a few isolated units. The pueblo contained over 100 rooms, 3 kivas, and several plazas. It was inhabited from the early 1300s to A.D. 1630. Joseph Toulouse excavated this site in 1941.

Two interesting sites are located on the west side of the Rio Grande in this area. These are Pottery Mound and the Gallinas Springs Site. **Pottery Mound** (LA 416) is situated on the west bank of the Rio Puerco, a tributary of the Rio Grande, southwest of the town of Los Lunas. This is a large Pueblo IV ruin that had unusually well-preserved kiva murals found by Frank Hibben during his excavations in 1954 to 1955 and 1957 to 1960. Some walls had many murals, one painted over another. These murals were carefully copied and reproduced by Frank C. Hibben, who authored a beautiful book with many color plates (1975).

Pottery Mound consists of three pueblos that were constructed at different times, one on top of the other. Some of them were three to four stories high. The pueblo was built on a flat-topped, pyramid-shaped mound, indicating possible influences from Mexico. The pueblos were constructed of puddled adobe walls surrounding four large plazas. Some of the painted kivas were almost square in shape. The site is named for the many types of pottery found here, including locally produced glaze-painted vessels. Unfortunately, this site has not been restored, and there is not much evidence of its interesting features. Pottery Mound was inhabited from the early 1300s to A.D. 1475.

Gallinas Springs Site (LA 1178) is in the northwest corner of Socorro County, New Mexico. It is located fifteen miles northwest of the town of Magdalena, in Cibola National Forest. The pueblo contained 500 masonry rooms that were arranged in a main "D"-shaped house block. Several other house blocks also were constructed. Some parts of the main structure were probably three stories high. The pueblo was excavated by personnel from Western Michigan University under the direction of Ernestine Green in 1974 to 1976, and some restoration was done. The site was inhabited from about A.D. 1250 to 1325.

To the south, east of the Rio Grande, about thirty miles north of Alamogordo, New Mexico, in the Tularosa Basin on the Old Fall Ranch, is **Three Rivers Ruin** (LA 1231). Three Rivers is a small pueblo ruin of about twelve rooms that was built about A.D. 1340. This site was excavated by C. B. Cosgrove in the early 1920s, but little was published on his findings.

There are some good petroglyphs nearby at **Three Rivers Petroglyphs,** * a Bureau of Land Management (BLM) site. This site has a small campground with restrooms but no drinking water. More than 500 petroglyphs can be seen along the top of a ridge. An asphalt trail about one mile in length leads past many prehistoric carvings. This easy hike takes about one hour. These petroglyphs were carved by people of the Jornada branch of the Mogollon culture about A.D. 900 to 1400. All of the sites in this area are Anasazi, or primarily Anasazi, except Three Rivers Ruin.

Map 5

Prehistoric Ruins of the Mimbres, Upper Gila and San Francisco River Valleys

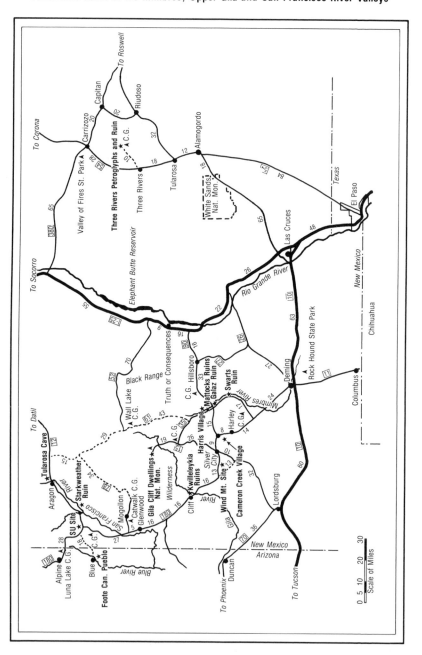

IV

The Mimbres, Upper Gila, and San Francisco River Valleys

These three rivers have their source in the mountains of southwestern New Mexico and flow through a sparsely settled and beautiful part of the Southwest. The Mimbres River flows between the Mimbres and Pinos Altos mountains in its upper stretches in a generally southern direction. North of the town of Deming, the river turns east, then disappears after leaving the Florida Mountains to the east. The Gila, the major drainage of this area, heads in the Mogollon Mountains, where it flows through scenic canyons in a virtual wilderness area. After leaving the mountains, it runs westerly to join the San Francisco River in eastern Arizona. The San Francisco flows out of the mountains of the same name near the town of Reserve, New Mexico. It runs south and then turns east toward the Blue Mountains of Arizona.

This is the heartland of the ancient Mogollon culture and all the sites described in this chapter are Mogollon, except Kwilleleykia which has Salado characteristics. The major town in this area is Silver City, New Mexico. It has good lodging and shopping facilities and is the location of Western New Mexico University, which has a small museum containing archeological materials from the vicinity.

Most of the ruins in the Mimbres Valley are on private land and have been "pothunted" for the beautiful and valuable black-on-white Mimbres pottery. Therefore, there are no restored ruins, and most of the sites are now low mounds covered with pot holes. Visitors must obtain permission from landowners to visit the ruins. Locations of the prehistoric sites in this area are shown on Map #5.

One Mimbres site that has survived and is under study can be visited at certain times, with permission. This is the **Wind Mountain Site*** (New Mexico:Y:7:1), which is being excavated by the Amerind Foundation of Dragoon, Arizona. This site is about ten miles southwest of Silver City, New Mexico, via U.S. Highway No. 180. You then travel south on an unpaved road for about one and one-half miles toward Wind Mountain in the Little Burro Mountains. The Wind Mountain Site and the adjacent **Ridout Site** (New Mexico:Y:7:3) comprise a multicomponent site of several superimposed Mogollon pithouse villages and a surface house village. The pithouse villages include two with round houses and two with rectangular houses. The surface structure is a group of masonry-walled, contiguous rooms. The local ceramics range in time from Alma Plain to Mimbres Classic Black-on-white, indicating occupation dates of circa A.D. 600 to 1,000. The wide variety of trade pottery indicates contact with Mesa Verde, Chaco, Hohokam, and Casas Grandes peoples.

This site may be visited and the excavations observed with prior permission. Information can be obtained from Dr. Charles C. DiPeso, Director, Amerind Foundation, Dragoon, Arizona 85609; telephone 602-586-3003.

Fortunately, the state of New Mexico has obtained a Mimbres site overlooking the Gila River near Silver City. This site, called **Mimbres State Monument,** consists of pithouses, masonry rooms, and possibly a great kiva. Occupation of this site ended about A.D. 1200. The ruin is now undeveloped, but it will be excavated and restored in the future so that the public will finally be able to see a Mimbres site. The Mimbres phase of the Mogollon culture existed from approximately A.D. 1075 to 1175.

Only three of the major Mimbres sites have been carefully excavated and the results published. These are Cameron Creek Village, the Swarts Ruin, and the Mattocks Ruin. The Galaz Ruin and Harris Village are also covered in this section, because information is available about them. Because of the almost total destruction of most Mimbres sites by vandals, there is much that will never be known about the Mimbres culture.

Cameron Creek Village (LA 190) is located on Cameron Creek, a western tributary of the Mimbres River. It is two miles west of Hurley, New Mexico. The ruin is situated on a short ridge that projects into the east side of Cameron Creek Valley. This site consisted of a village of forty pithouses and a great lodge or kiva-type structure. Wesley Bradfield excavated a total of 138 rooms in 1923 to 1928, and his 1931 publication has many illustrations of the fine pottery found at this site. Cameron Creek Village was occupied from about A.D. 700 to an undetermined date. Camping is available nearby at City of Rocks State Park, twenty-eight miles north of Deming, New Mexico, via Highway No. 180.

Another ruin located in the bottom of the Mimbres River valley on the Swarts Ranch is named the **Swarts Ruin** (LA 1691). It was occupied from A.D. 950 to 1175 and covers an area of 268 by 300 feet. It is fifteen miles south of the town of Mimbres. There are about 172 total rooms, some of which are early one-room pithouses. There are two house blocks of masonry rooms of stone and adobe totaling 125 rooms from the final occupation. Each house block had one large ceremonial room, and there were four enclosed plazas. The population in the last phase of occupation has been estimated at 175 persons.

Mr. and Mrs. C. B. Cosgrove excavated Swarts Ruin in 1924 to 1927 and published a complete report in 1932. A good summary of this site is found in a recent book on Mimbres pottery by J. J. Brody (1977). More than 1,000 pottery vessels were found at Swarts Ruin, mostly from the 1,009 burials uncovered. Swarts Ruin is now leveled.

In the vicinity of the small settlement of Mimbres, New Mexico, are three well-known excavated ruins. These are the Mattocks Ruin, the Galaz Ruin, and Harris Village.

Mattocks Ruin (LA 676) is in the Upper Mimbres Valley about one mile south of the Mimbres post office. It is situated on a level terrace above the west bank of the Mimbres River. The ruin is constructed of adobe and stone and consisted of 192 rooms in four room blocks. The site was occupied from Pueblo I to early Pueblo III times. It was excavated in 1929 to 1930 by Paul Nesbitt.

Galaz Ruin (LA 635) is about five miles south of the Mimbres post office. It is on a terrace above the arroyo cut by the Mimbres River. Galaz was partially excavated by the Southwest Museum in 1927. Four pithouses roughly circular in shape with plastered and baked walls were excavated. The ruin spanned two time periods and had two connected tiers of pueblo rooms superimposed on a lower row of partly subterranean, masonry-lined rooms. The Galaz Ruin is on property owned by the Galaz family, and it has been pothunted and recently bulldozed until little remains.

On the east bank of the Mimbres River, one-fourth mile east of the Mimbres post office, is the site known as **Harris Village** (LA 1867). It is situated on a portion of a large, flat terrace that rises abruptly to a height of twenty meters. The area of occupation was several acres. Harris Village was a settlement of well over 100 pithouses, of which 34 were excavated by Emil Haury in 1934. The pithouses varied considerably in shape due to several phases of construction.

Other named Mimbres sites include **Old Town Ruin, Osborn Ruin, Mimbres Site, Ft. Bayard (Whiskey Creek) Site, Mangas Springs**, and **Hurley Site**.

North of the Mimbres Valley in the Gila National Forest is **Gila Cliff Dwellings National Monument**.* The monument is forty-seven miles north of Silver City, New Mexico, via New Mexico No. 15 and No. 35. There is no public transportation to the monument. The ruins are located in a small canyon on the West Fork of the Gila River. A half-mile trail leads over the stream and up the

Masonry rooms in caves at Gila Cliff Dwellings National Monument, New Mexico

canyon to the ruins, built in large caves 180 feet above the canyon floor. Regular guided tours and weekend campfire talks are given by national monument personnel.

The major ruin is a multicomponent site consisting of five caves with masonry rooms. The largest cave is fifty feet in diameter and ten feet high and has a one-room structure. Two of the smaller caves have stone and adobe rooms. Several of the caves are connected. In the five caves, forty rooms were built of rock with adobe plaster, some of which remains today. There are pictographs on the walls of some of the caves. Other small ruins are located in nearby canyons.

A separate site known as **T J Pueblo** is located on a mesa above the visitors' center. Plans have been made to excavate and stabilize this ruin so that it may be seen in the future.

The "excavation" of Gila Cliff Dwellings consisted primarily of early pothunting, and little scientific study has been carried out. Gordon Vivian did some excavation and stabilization in 1955 and 1963, but no comprehensive report on this site has been published. The best source of written information is a popular booklet by Elizabeth McFarland published in 1967. The ruins at this site are some of the least studied of any of our national monuments.

T-shaped door at Gila Cliff Dwellings shows Anasazi influence at this Mogollon site

Masonry room tucked into cave at Gila Cliff Dwellings

The prehistoric inhabitants of Gila Cliff Dwellings were Mogollon, but Anasazi influences from the north, such as the "T"-shaped doorways, are also present. These cliff dwellings were inhabited from circa A.D. 1290 to 1450.

Gila Cliff Dwellings National Monument has a small visitors' center and a campground, both of which are open year-round. No lodging, food, gas, or other services are available at the monument, but a private dude ranch is located nearby. The ruins are inaccessible to persons in wheelchairs, but the visitors' center can be reached.

This monument is in a rather out-of-the-way place, but it is definitely worth visiting, particularly if you can combine seeing the ruins with a hike or backpack trip into the beautiful Gila Wilderness Area that surrounds the monument. This is one of the most scenic and appealing wild spots in the Southwest, and it is uncrowded most of the year.

Near the town of Cliff, New Mexico, on U.S. Highway No. 180, are the little-known **Kwilleleykia Ruins*** (LA 4935). This site is privately owned by Mr. and Mrs. Richard "Red" Ellison of Silver

City. Mr. Ellison has been excavating at Kwilleleykia for fourteen years, and his knowledge of this ruin and others in the Silver City vicinity is extensive. He has interesting theories about the prehistoric inhabitants of the Mimbres and Upper Gila valleys. Mr. Ellison is willing to spend time answering questions of interested visitors. His address is Box 918, Silver City, New Mexico 88061. His work at Kwilleleykia has preserved much from an important site that would otherwise have been leveled for agriculture. This ruin is easy to reach and should be seen while passing through the area.

Kwilleleykia is a short distance east of Cliff, and directional signs in town lead to the site. The ruin is on the floodplain of the Gila River in an arable spot. It consists of three room blocks, totaling 300 rooms, and two large plaza areas. There is also a large "ceremonial room" that contains several fire pits. Part of the pueblo has been excavated, and the small visitors' center contains pottery and other artifacts from the site.

Excavations at Kwilleylekia Ruins show difficulty of maintaining adobe walls

The prehistoric inhabitants were apparently Salado. This is the most easterly of the large Salado sites. The final inhabitants may have moved to Hawikuh near the present Zuni Pueblo. Kwilleleykia was inhabited from about A.D. 1425 to 1575. A flood covered part of the pueblo in the later years.

The site is open from 8:00 AM to 6:00 PM in the summer, and a small fee is charged for adults. Excavations can be observed when

Mr. Ellison or his assistants are working and the site is easily accessible to wheelchairs. The Catwalk Campground is near the town of Glenwood, north of Cliff on U.S. Highway No. 180.

To the north, in the vicinity of Reserve, New Mexico, are a number of excavated sites, many of which were dug by the Field Museum of Chicago under the direction of Paul Martin.

Three and one-half miles east of Reserve in Gila National Forest is the **Starkweather Ruin,** which was excavated in 1935 to 1936 by Paul Nesbitt. The report of this work was published by Nesbitt in 1938. Starkweather is a village of deep circular pithouses, some with entrances in the roofs. A "great lodge" had a diameter of thirty-seven feet and was five feet in depth. This structure was circular in shape and had a side entrance. Starkweather is a Mogollon site, and tree-ring dates indicate that it was inhabited in A.D. 927.

In the foothills of the San Francisco Mountains, atop a ridge in Gila National Forest, is the **SU Site.** It is seven miles west of Reserve, New Mexico. This site is an early Mogollon village of twenty-eight excavated pithouses. The houses were constructed of logs and were chinked with mud and branches. Many storage pits and fire pits were found in the houses. Several of the houses were unusually large and may have been used for ceremonial purposes. An immense variety of artifacts was found during the excavation by Paul Martin in 1939 and from 1945 to 1946. This village was occupied from circa A.D. 300 to 500. Today the site consists of depressions and sherd areas on the ridge top.

Another well-known site in this area is **Tularosa Cave** (LA 4427). It is located in Apache National Forest, Catron County, New Mexico, and is one mile east of Aragon on New Mexico Highway No. 12 between Reserve and Datil. The cave is situated on the north side of Tularosa Canyon.

At the mouth of the cave were a row of pueblo masonry rooms. Petroglyphs are present on the cliff face adjacent to the cave. The floor of the cave is twelve by eight meters, and twelve small pits were found during excavations. Martin excavated Tularosa Cave in 1950 for the Field Museum of Natural History. Many perishable artifacts of scientific value were found in the dry refuse of this site. This cave was occupied intermittently for approximately 1,500 years—from 400 B.C. to A.D. 1100.

Many other sites are located in the Reserve area of the San Francisco River valley, but few have been scientifically excavated, and none have been restored. This is probably due to the sparse

contemporary population in the region and the fact that pithouse
architecture does not lend itself to impressive restorations.

Exterior of restored painted kiva at Kuaua Pueblo, Coronado
State Monument, New Mexico

Map 6

Prehistoric Ruins of the White Mts. and Upper Salt River Valley

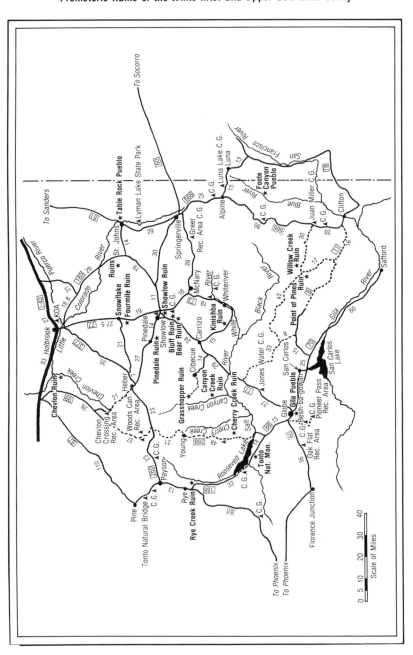

V

White Mountain and Upper Salt River Area

T his area in east-central Arizona, most of which is on the Fort Apache and San Carlos Indian reservations, is a fine place for outdoor vacations and contains many prehistoric ruins. Numerous campgrounds are located in the mountain sections, and fairly good trout fishing is available in the lakes and in a few streams. A tribal permit is required to camp or fish on the reservations. There are lodging accommodations at Springerville, McNary, and Show Low in the northeast section and at Globe and Miami in the southeast.

This area extends from Springerville, Arizona, in the east to Snowflake in the north and Roosevelt Lake in the southwest. It includes most of the Upper Salt River and its tributaries to the north and a small portion of the Little Colorado watershed over the divide to the north. The elevation of this area varies from 10,000 feet in the White Mountains to 5,000 feet in the Miami–Globe vicinity. This area contains prehistoric remains of all three of the major prehistoric cultures: Anasazi, Mogollon and Hohokam and also encompasses nearly all of the area of the Salado, a minor group. The locations of the sites in this area are shown on Map #6.

The major excavated and restored ruins are Kinishba near Whitewater, Besh-ba-gowah and Gila Pueblo at Globe, and Tonto

National Monument near Roosevelt Lake. Grasshopper Ruin near Cibecue, Arizona, has been under excavation by summer field schools from the University of Arizona since 1963, and visitors will find it very instructive to observe the work of archeologists in progress.

Twenty miles west of Reserve, New Mexico, in Arizona's Apache National Forest, at the confluence of Foote Creek and the Blue River, is **Foote Canyon Pueblo** (LA 4425). It is in Sitgreaves National Forest, about three miles south of the Blue post office, and is situated on a low, rocky mesa. The original mound at this ruin was 130 feet by 90 feet in size. This ruin has five house blocks in the vicinity of a large, rectangular kiva. Twelve rooms and a plaza were excavated by John Rinaldo in 1955. Foote Canyon was occupied from A.D. 1245 to 1350. A good campground and fishing are available at Luna Lake near Alpine, Arizona.

Kinishba Ruin* (LA 1895) is in Gila County, Arizona, on the Fort Apache Indian Reservation. It is located eight miles southwest of Whiteriver, Arizona, on Arizona Highway No. 73, and one mile north on a dirt road.

This ruin is an Anasazi and Mogollon, Pueblo III structure occupied from A.D. 1250 to 1325. It is composed of two large

Damaged corner of masonry pueblo, Kinishba Ruin, Fort Apache Indian Reservation

Detail of masonry wall showing thin spalls between main building blocks, Kinishba Ruin

units, each containing about 200 rooms. Outlying units bring the total number of rooms to 500, which may have housed 1,000 to 2,000 persons. This ruin was excavated and restored by Byron Cummings in 1931 to 1939. Unfortunately, the site has not been well maintained and is falling into ruin again. In spite of this, Kinishba is one of the best restored examples of a pueblo ruin in this area. Several campgrounds are located northeast of Whiteriver.

In the vicinity of Forestdale Valley, on the Fort Apache Reservation, are several other sites, three of which are Bear Ruin, Bluff Ruin, and Forestdale Ruin. Directions and permission to visit these ruins should be sought at the White Mountain Apache tribal headquarters in the town of Whiteriver.

Bear Ruin (Ariz. P:16:1 ASM) is in Forestdale Valley, one mile south of the Forestdale Trading Post. It is situated on the highest of five terraces on the east bank of Forestdale Creek.

The ruin consists of thirteen round and square pithouses, storage rooms, and one great kiva. Burials were found in shallow pits throughout the village. Bear Ruin was occupied circa A.D. 641 to 713 and was excavated by Emil Haury in 1940.

Near to Bear Ruin is **Bluff Ruin** (Ariz. P:16:20 ASM), located one and one-half miles south of the Forestdale Trading Post. It is situated on a bluff east of Forestdale Valley. Bluff is an early pithouse village of twenty-three houses and a great kiva. The site was occupied from A.D. 238 to 322 and was excavated by Emil Haury and Ted Sayles in 1941 and 1944.

On the left bank of Forestdale Creek, a few hundred yards downstream from Bear Ruin, is **Forestdale Ruin** (NA 999). It is one mile southeast of the Forestdale Trading Post. Forestdale is a twenty-two room masonry pueblo with a circular great kiva twenty-five meters southwest of the room block. It was inhabited later than the Bear and Bluff sites, probably from A.D. 1080 to 1115. Emil Haury excavated Forestdale in 1939.

North of Forestdale are two well-known ruins in the Pinedale–Show Low area.

Show Low Ruin (NA 1003), also called **Whipple Ruin,** is located in southern Navajo County. It is actually in the town of Show Low, Arizona, on the west side of Show Low Creek, a tributary of Silver Creek. Show Low is a masonry pueblo of approximately 200 rooms. Most of the pueblo was burned in the late fourteenth century. There were two occupations, the first from A.D. 1200 to 1300 and the second from A.D. 1335 to 1384. Emil Haury excavated twenty-nine rooms at Show Low in 1929.

Sixteen miles west of Show Low Ruin and one-half mile southeast of the town of Pinedale, Arizona, is **Pinedale Ruin** (NA 1006). Pinedale is a large, hollow, rectangular pueblo constructed of chinked, dressed stone masonry. It consists of approximately 200 rooms and one kiva and covers an area of 250 feet by 250 feet. This ruin was occupied from A.D. 1275 to 1325. Jesse Fewkes did some excavation here in 1897, and Emil Haury dug more extensively in 1929. This ruin is on private property, and in recent years it has been dug extensively for pottery. In 1980, the owner was building a home on the site.

Further north in Navajo County is **Fourmile Ruin** (NA 1005), located on the west bank of Cottonwood Creek about four miles south of Snowflake, Arizona. It is situated on a bluff overlooking Cottonwood Creek. Fourmile is a large, rectangular pueblo with a central plaza at the western end. A number of burials were found in cemeteries on the north and south sides. The single date for this ruin is A.D. 1380. The site was partially excavated by Jesse Fewkes in 1897 and is best known for a widely traded type of pottery called Fourmile Polychrome. Fourmile Polychrome has a red base color with striking black geometric designs outlined by narrow white lines.

Grasshopper Ruin* (ASM:P:14:1) is located in southern Navajo County, Arizona, about fifteen miles west of the small Apache town of Cibecue. The ruin is in a pine forest on an old lava flow. The two units comprising the ruin are separated by the Salt River draw.

Grasshopper is a large ruin of 500 rooms in 13 room blocks and outlying rooms. The walls were constructed of sandstone masonry, and some portions were two stories in height. The University of Arizona field schools have been excavating here since 1963. In addition to the many rooms, several small, rectangular kivas and one rectangular great kiva have been excavated. Many burials have also been excavated.

Grasshopper was occupied from about A.D. 1200 to 1400. Visitors are permitted to observe the excavations in progress during the summer months. No public lodging or camping facilities are available at the site, but there is camping to the east on the Fort Apache Indian Reservation.

Southwest of Grasshopper are several ruins in isolated canyons that are tributary to the Salt River.

Canyon Creek Ruin (Ariz. C:2:8GP) is in Gila County, Arizona, in the canyon of Canyon Creek, one mile below the mouth of Oak Creek, an eastern tributary. It is also within the boundaries of the Tonto National Forest. The ruin is 1,000 feet above the creek in a small box canyon and lies under an overhanging sandstone cliff. The only way to reach this ruin is by foot or horseback from the dirt road that parallels Canyon Creek on the east. Visitors are discouraged from trying to find it without a local guide.

The ruin is a cliff dwelling of fifty-eight rooms built of slab masonry, chinked with mud and stone spalls. Part of the ruin was probably two stories in height. Outlying rooms are scattered about the base of the cliff and in surrounding canyons. Harold S.Gladwin excavated Canyon Creek Ruin in the early 1930s and found a large, clay-covered storage basket and textiles among the artifacts. Canyon Creek was occupied from A.D. 1323 to 1350, when this site and others in the area were apparently abandoned.

Sierra Ancha Ruin (Ariz. C:1:16), also known as Pueblo Canyon, is located in Pueblo Canyon a few hundred yards west of Canyon Creek Ruin. It is situated in a cave in the north wall of the canyon. Sierra Ancha is composed of three small groups of masonry rooms totaling sixty to seventy-five rooms. The site was occupied from A.D. 1278 to 1324. Several smaller cliff dwellings of three to fifteen rooms are located near Sierra Ancha.

Overlooking Roosevelt Lake in Gila County, Arizona, is **Tonto National Monument**,* established in 1907. The monument is twenty-eight miles north of Globe, Arizona, via Arizona Highway No. 88. It is northeast of Phoenix via U.S. Highway No. 60 and Arizona Highway No. 88 at Apache Junction. The monument visitors' center is two miles southeast of Roosevelt, in Cholla Canyon. The monument is open year-round from 8:00 AM to 5:00 PM. The address of the monument superintendent is P.O. Box 707, Roosevelt, Arizona 85545.

The total area of the monument is one and one-half square miles. The ruins are cliff dwellings built into three caves. They are known as **Lower Ruin** (nineteen rooms), **Lower Ruin Annex** (eleven rooms), and **Upper Ruin** (forty rooms). Upper Ruin is 250 feet above the lower portions. The walls are constructed of unshaped quartzite stone laid in adobe mortar. The Upper Ruin was excavated by Charlie Steen in 1940, and Lloyd M. Pierson excavated the Lower Ruin and the Annex in 1950. Among the artifacts recovered were many textiles and other interesting perishables, some of which are exhibited in the visitors' center.

Salado people built masonry rooms in this cave, Lower Ruins, Tonto National Monument, Arizona

Walls built around a large boulder at Lower Ruins,
Tonto National Monument

Tonto Ruin is one of the major centers of the Salado branch of the Mogollon. The site was occupied circa A.D. 1350 to 1400. In 1400, all of the sites in this area were abandoned. Tonto is an outstanding restored ruin and is a pleasant place for a short visit, particularly in the months from October to June. There is a half-mile, self-guided hike to the Lower Ruin. Along the trail are signs pointing out the native plants, including several types of cactus. This trail is not recommended for wheelchairs or persons with respiratory conditions. Hikes to the Upper Ruin must be arranged five days in advance with the resident ranger. No campsites are available at the monument, but a campground is located nearby at Roosevelt Lake, and lodging is available at Miami or Globe, Arizona.

Rye Creek Ruin (Ariz. 15:1), northeast of Tonto National Monument in Tonto National Forest, is on the west bank of Rye Creek at its junction with Deer Creek. It is a medium-sized masonry ruin of over 200 rooms in the shape of an arc. The ends of the arc are joined by a wall to form a large court. The walls are constructed of river boulders laid up in mud. Harold S. Gladwin excavated here in 1930 and found many slab-lined storage pits but no kivas or other ceremonial rooms. Rye Creek Ruin has been badly pothunted in the past and is carefully protected by Tonto National Forest archeologists.

A number of sites were inundated by the filling of Roosevelt Lake. One of these is the well-known site designated **Roosevelt 9:6.** It is not situated below the high-water mark of the lake on the old bank of the Salt River, about four miles east of Tonto National Monument. This site was a Hohokam village of fourteen houses. Two posts held a center roof beam in each house. Walls were built of smaller poles covered with branches, reeds, and mud. All of the burials excavated by Emil Haury in 1931 were cremations. The village was inhabited from A.D. 700 to 900. Obviously, this site cannot be visited unless you have scuba equipment.

Besh-ba-gowah Pueblo* is owned by the city of Globe, Arizona. To reach it, follow Broad Street about one mile from the center of Globe, cross the second bridge over Pinal Creek, and proceed one-half mile up Six Shooter Canyon to a marked access road on the right. A sign that says "Globe Community Center" marks the short gravel road up to the ruin.

This pueblo ruin of approximately 200 rooms covered an area of two acres. Besh-ba-gowah means "metal camp" in the Apache language, and this site was occupied from A.D. 1225 to 1400. The masonry pueblo was excavated and partially restored under the direction of Irene Vickery in 1938 but has been left open to the elements and is falling into disrepair.

This Salado site is open all year, at all hours.

Other ruins are located along Pinal Creek in this vicinity. A small museum is housed at the Globe city hall, and a picnic ground and swimming pool are also by the city hall building. Accommodations are available in Globe, and campgrounds can be found a few miles south of town at Pinal Mountain and Pioneer Pass.

One mile beyond Besh-ba-gowah on the west bank of Pinal Creek, in Six Shooter Canyon, is **Gila Pueblo.*** This site was excavated and partially restored beginning in 1928. Part of the prehistoric structure was rebuilt and turned into a modern museum by the noted archeologist Harold S. Gladwin. For many years this was an active center of southwestern archeological surveys and other research. It is now inactive, and the collections have been moved to the Arizona State Museum. In 1972, Gila Pueblo College was opened in the museum facilities. This institution is a community

Besh-ba-gowah Pueblo, Globe, Arizona, low doorway topped by wooden lintel

college serving the people of the Globe–Miami area. In the court-yard south of the main building, several excavated and stabilized rooms of the original pueblo may be seen, and a few artifacts are exhibited in the college building.

Gila Pueblo was a typical late Salado pueblo of 225 rooms. The walls were built of boulders plastered with mud. Most of these rooms had been burned. Harold Gladwin excavated 200 rooms at Gila. The pueblo was built in A.D. 1325 and burned about A.D. 1385. A good campground is located at San Carlos Lake southeast of Globe. A warning—this area can be very hot in the summer months!

Near **Point of Pines** (Ariz. W:10:50), sixty-five miles east of Globe, Arizona, on the San Carlos Apache Indian Reservation, is a ruin of the same name. It is on Point of Pines Creek, east of Point of Pines on the south side of the road. This ruin was excavated by University of Arizona archeology summer field schools for about ten years beginning in 1947 under the direction of Emil Haury. It is one of the very few sites where evidence of the three major cultures of the Southwest—Anasazi, Hohokam, and Mogollon—are found contemporaneously. Some of the burials found during the exca-

Walls of excavated Salado room in courtyard at Gila Pueblo
College, Globe, Arizona

vations were cremations indicating influences from the Hohokam
where this was the usual method of interment. Another Hohokam
trait was the finely done decorations on shell and bone articles. The
architecture of the pueblos and the kivas, and the designs on some
of the painted pottery give evidence of infusion of traits from the
Kayenta Branch of the Anasazi. The basic utility pottery at Point of
Pines is a brown type characteristic of the Mogollon to the east.

The main ruin was a masonry pueblo of about 800 rooms.
There are also other room blocks built at various times. The main
ruin had a great wall surrounding it, a plaza, and a great kiva.
Many burials and artifacts were recovered during the excavations.
The ruin was occupied from A.D. 1200 to 1500 with the peak population around A.D. 1300. No walls are presently standing at Point
of Pines, but extensive ruins of walls and excavated areas are still
visible.

Five miles east of Point of Pines is **Willow Creek Ruin** (Ariz.
W:10:105). It is on the north rim of Willow Creek Canyon east of
the point where Willow Creek enters Willow Creek Canyon. It is
on an old lava flow on the San Carlos Apache Indian Reservation.
This ruin is divided into northern and southern units by a plaza.

Walls on the east and west sides connect these units. The northern unit had forty-five rooms, and the southern unit had fifteen rooms and a possible kiva. Willow Creek Ruin was occupied from A.D. 1400 to 1450, and one room and two stone ring structures were excavated by Emil Haury in 1956. Outlines of walls are still visible among the large amounts of fallen building stones.

Information and directions to prehistoric ruins on the San Carlos Apache Indian Reservation can be obtained at the tribal headquarters of the San Carlos Apache tribe in the town of San Carlos, twenty-five miles east of Globe, Arizona.

Map 7

Prehistoric Ruins of the Middle Gila and Salt River

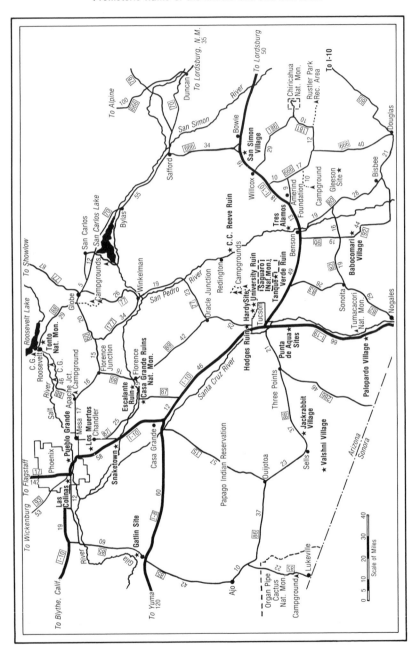

VI

The Middle Gila and Salt River Area

T his area is in the desert country of southern Arizona and is best visited in the winter months. There are many air-conditioned motels in the Phoenix area, and these are recommended for those who do not have air-cooled recreational vehicles for the hot summer months.

This region includes the lower stretches of the Salt River where it flows through the Phoenix metropolitan area to the confluence of the Salt with the Gila River, west of Phoenix. It also includes the valleys of three southern tributaries of the Gila River that drain most of southeastern Arizona. These streams are the Santa Cruz, the San Pedro, and the San Simon. They are all usually dry and only flow during the infrequent desert rains.

The three excavated and restored ruins in this area, which was once well populated by the Hohokam, are Pueblo Grande in Phoenix, Casa Grande near Coolidge, Arizona, and the Hardy Site in Tucson. Most of the remaining sites in this area have been leveled for agriculture or urban development. Those that do exist are evidenced only by low mounds and scattered potsherds. One of the outstanding characteristics of the Hohokam was their extensive irrigation systems that enabled them to exist in this arid country. Little evidence remains of many miles of prehistoric canals, because modern building has obliterated most of them. Some of the modern canals and ditches in the Salt River Valley follow those of the ancient Hohokam. The locations of the Hohokam sites described in this chapter are shown on Map #7.

Visitors to Phoenix should be certain to see the Heard Museum at 22 East Monte Vista Road. This is an outstanding institution, and all persons interested in the prehistoric Southwest will enjoy viewing the exhibits. The major displays include the Pueblo Gallery, the Spanish Colonial Room, the Gallery of Indian Art, the Southwestern Silver display and the Prehistory of the Southwest exhibit. A gift shop sells Indian arts and crafts and books on the Southwest. The museum is open from 10:00 AM to 5:00 PM, Monday through Saturday, and 1:00 PM to 5:00 PM on Sundays.

A number of good Indian arts and crafts stores are located in the Phoenix suburb of Scottsdale.

Pueblo Grande,* located in Phoenix at 4619 East Washington Street, near the airport, is the excavated and partially restored remains of a Hohokam village built on a large mound. It includes a restored ball court and the remains of irrigation canals. The houses were constructed of poles that were covered with brush and plastered with mud. The earthen platform upon which the houses were built is held in place by retaining walls. The ball court has been

Heard Museum, Phoenix, Arizona

Excavations of Hohokam structures and museum at Pueblo
Grande, Phoenix, Arizona

Excavations viewed from observation tower, Pueblo Grande

73

completely excavated and is eighty-five feet long and forty-one feet wide. It has been reconstructed with cement. Some of the Hohokam canals in this area were very deep and were lined with clay to prevent seepage. Pueblo Grande dates from circa A.D. 1200 to 1400.

A small museum houses a good selection of well-exhibited artifacts that were found at Pueblo Grande. The present modern museum was dedicated in 1974; it includes several research laboratories and a library. Excavation began at Pueblo Grande in the 1930s and has continued intermittently to the present. Pueblo Grande is administered by the division of archeology of the city of Phoenix. Visitors may take a short self-guided tour over the mound, and staff members are available for group lectures. The museum is accessible to disabled persons, but the ruins are not. The best view of the mound is obtained by ascending a wooden observation tower near the center of the mound. The museum is open from 9:00 AM to 5:00 PM during the week and from 1:00 PM to 4:45 PM on Sunday. The telephone number is 602-275-3452. Pueblo Grande is a good site to visit when in Phoenix and when time is limited.

About six and one-half miles south of the center of Tempe, Arizona, is the Hohokam village known as **Los Muertos** (Ariz. U:9:56). It was a large village of twenty-five to thirty house groups totaling over one thousand rooms. The original settlement has been estimated to have been one-half to one mile wide and five miles long. This site was occupied from A.D. 1300 to 1400 and was probably the largest of the twenty some Hohokam villages in this area of the Salt River valley. Los Muertos was named for the many burials, both cremations and inhumations, found here during the excavations. Four hundred rooms of this site were excavated by the Hemenway Expedition in 1887 to 1888 under the direction of Frank H. Cushing. The complete results of this work were not reported until they were published by Emil Haury in 1945. This great site has been nearly obliterated by farming and encroaching housing developments. It is located on private land, and nothing remains to see of this once great Hohokam village.

Several other large Hohokam villages were located near Los Muertos when the Europeans arrived in this area. Four other sites to the north of Los Muertos, all of which had some early excavation and have since been destroyed, are **Las Acequias, Los Guancos, Los Hornos,** and **Pueblo de las Canopas (Pueblo Viejo).**

Another excavated site in the city of Phoenix is **Las Colinas**

(Ariz. T:12:10). It is west of downtown Phoenix in an area bounded by Nineteenth Avenue and Twenty-Seventh Avenue on the east and west, respectively, and by Thomas Road on the north and Van Buren Street on the south. The original site consisted of twelve large mounds. One of these was a platform mound built of adobe retaining walls filled with rubble. A large village of pithouses and rectangular surface rooms encircles the mounds. Excavations revealed both cremations and inhumations at this site. Ten of the mounds have been leveled for building, and only the base remains of one mound. Mound No. 8 was saved because an adobe house was built on it in the 1880s. This site was excavated by Laurens C. Hammack in 1969. Part of this site is on private land, and the remainder is land owned by the Arizona Department of Transportation.

The most extensively studied and reported site in this area is **Snaketown** (Ariz. U:13:1). Snaketown lies on the Gila River Indian Reservation about twelve miles southwest of Chandler, Arizona, and is the same distance west-northwest of Sacaton. It is on the north bank of the Gila River, five miles west of the point where Interstate 10 crosses the river.

Snaketown was a large Hohokam village, one-half by three-fourths miles in dimension and covering an area of 250 acres. The abandoned site was composed of 60 low mounds. The many houses were scattered over the area in a somewhat random pattern. The typical square or rectangular house had walls and a roof of reeds supported by an internal structure of posts. It was covered on the outside with mud. A covered entrance was located on the long side of the house. Nothing remains of these prehistoric houses except the hard-packed floors found during excavation.

A total of 206 rooms were excavated at Snaketown, 40 by Harold S. Gladwin in 1934 to 1945 and 166 by Emil Haury in 1964 to 1965. The sixty mounds were of three types—some were trash mounds, others were earth mounds used as building platforms, and some were combinations of the first two types. Two ball courts were also found, in addition to eight crematory areas with elonged depressions used as crematoria. Snaketown was occupied for 700 years from A.D. 300 to 1000. Snaketown was declared a registered national historic landmark and in 1972 became part of the national park system.

The excavations have been backfilled, so there is not much to see at Snaketown today. Nevertheless, it is interesting to walk over the site and examine the environment. A small historic Pima Indian village existed on part of the site, and a few evidences of this occupation remain. An interesting model of the Snaketown site has been prepared at the Heard Museum in Phoenix. Most of the artifacts excavated at Snaketown are now housed in the Arizona State Museum.

The excavations at Snaketown have been reported in an excellent University of Arizona publication (Haury, 1976).

Thirty miles upstream from Snaketown and three miles northwest of Florence on the north side of the Gila River is a Hohokam site known as **Escalante Ruin** (Ariz. U:15:3). It consists of a compound of jacal surface rooms and a platform mound. The rooms were arranged in rows and housed about seventy-five people. It was occupied from A.D. 100 to 1450 and was excavated in 1973 by David E. Doyel. This site is on land owned by the Continental Oil Company and is scheduled to become an open-pit mine.

Casa Grande Ruins National Monument* is located two miles south of Chandler, Arizona, on Arizona Highway No. 87. It is about halfway between Phoenix and Tucson. The address is Coolidge, Arizona 85228.

The monument covers 427 acres and includes the remains of several Hohokam villages. The Casa Grande structure itself is a large, four-story building constructed of coursed caliche. The structure is forty by sixty feet in size and is thirty feet in height. It contained eleven rooms. The use of this unusual building is unknown, but it may have served as an astronomical observatory. The monument also includes the remains of a system of irrigation canals. Casa Grande was named by Father Kino in 1694. The dates of occupation for Casa Grande are A.D. 1350 to 1450.

The first excavations at this site were conducted by Cosmos Mindeleff in 1891. He cleared the fill out of the rooms and did some stabilization. Other excavations were carried out from 1906 to 1908, in 1928, in 1930, and in recent years by National Park Service personnel. In 1932, the Park Service built a large roof over the ruin to protect it from further weathering.

The visitor may take a self-guided trail around the ruin or a conducted tour. The visitors' center contains artifacts from the site. Casa Grande has a picnic ground but no overnight camping facilities. The monument is entirely accessible to wheelchairs. Lodging accommodations are available at Coolidge, Arizona. The monument is open year-round from 8:00 AM to 5:00 PM. It is best to visit Casa Grande during the months from October to June.

Southeast of Phoenix in the vicinity of Tucson, Arizona, and to the east in the valleys of the San Pedro and San Simon are a number of Hohokam sites surveyed and excavated by the University of Arizona at Tucson and the Amerind Foundation at Dragoon, Arizona. Unfortunately, none of these sites have been restored.

Tucson is the major town in southeastern Arizona, and it is a good place to stay while visiting this area. Several campgrounds are located in the Catalina Mountains to the northeast of Tucson.

The **Arizona State Museum** at the University of Arizona provides exhibits and study materials of great interest to those who want to learn more about the Hohokam and other cultures of the prehistoric Southwest. The museum, located at Park Avenue and University Boulevard, is open 10:00 AM to 5:00 PM, Monday through Saturday, and 2:00 PM to 5:00 PM on Sundays. The telephone number is 602-626-1180.

The **Amerind Foundation** is a private archeological research institution. It maintains a small, but excellent, museum and laboratory at the small town of Dragoon, Arizona, located sixty-five miles southeast of Tucson on Interstate 10. It is recommended that you call prior to visiting the museum to be certain that staff will be available to conduct a tour. The address and telephone number of the Amerind Foundation are Dragoon, Arizona 85609; 602-586-3003. The museum contains a fine collection of prehistoric and historic material, primarily from southern Arizona and northern Mexico. Personnel of this institution have recently concluded extensive excavations of the huge prehistoric site at **Casas Grandes**,* Chihuahua, Mexico. This work has been reported in a multivolume publication authored by Charles C. DiPeso, director of the Amerind Foundation.

University Ruin (Ariz. BB:9:33) is northeast of Tucson on the lower east terrace of Pantano Wash. The ruin extends for some distance along and back of the terrace edge. The main mound, owned by the University of Arizona, has a caretaker and is surrounded by a fence. The area around the site is a housing subdivision known as Indian Ridge Estates.

This ruin consisted of a group of single-storied surface rooms and pithouses. The caliche walls were reinforced with posts. Several large mounds were the remains of filled-in rooms or multistoried structures of some complexity. University Ruin was excavated from 1930 to 1933 by Byron Cummings and in the late 1930s by Emil Haury; it was occupied from about A.D. 1200 to 1400.

Another site in the Tucson area, and the only one that has

Partially restored pithouse with replaced posts and outline of walls, Hardy Site, Tucson, Arizona

been restored, is the **Hardy Site** * (Ariz. GG:9:11), in Fort Lowell County Park. This large Hohokam village once covered most of the area now occupied by the park. This Tucson Basin Hohokam village was inhabited from circa A.D. 900 to 1300. In 1974, W. Bruce Masse and Gordon L. Fritz of the Arizona State Museum carried out test excavations that indicated four pithouses and several trash deposits. In 1976, the museum mapped and excavated an area east of Fort Lowell Park. The map shows several trash mounds, sherd areas, and an historic irrigation canal and trash dump.

Today this site contains a partially restored rectangular pithouse outlined by a low curb. The main house posts have been replaced. The house had a rectangular entryway on the north side. It is one of the very few restored pithouses in the Hohokam area. The site has interpretive signs, which makes it a good place to visit when in Tucson. Fort Lowell County Park is in northeastern Tucson on Fort Lowell Road near its junction with Craycroft Road, southwest of Pantano Wash.

Another well-known site in this area is **Hodges Ruin** (Ariz. AA:12:18), located seven miles northwest of Tucson near the confluence of Rillito Creek and the Santa Cruz River. Most of this site is now covered by a mobile home park that is adjacent to a gravel pit. This site originally covered nearly sixty acres. Hodges Ruin is a Hohokam village of eighty-four pithouses of five different types and a ball court similar to the one at Snaketown. It was excavated by Isabell T. Kelly for Gila Pueblo from 1937 to 1938. The prehistoric occupation of this village was from A.D. 300 to 1300.

South of Tucson and two and one-half miles south of the Mission San Xavier del Bac on the San Xavier Indian Reservation are the **Punta de Agua Sites** (Ariz. BB:13:16,41,43,50). These sites are located on ridges between arroyos or on the upper terrace of the earlier west channel of the Santa Cruz River. There are ten groups of houses, four of which were excavated by James Scisenti and J. Cameron Greenleaf in 1965 to 1966. The houses were rectangular, oval, or square in shape with entrances on the long side. A total of sixty-one living units were excavated in the four house groups. These houses were built without any significant excavation and therefore cannot be considered true pithouses. The village was inhabited from A.D. 900 to 1215. Some of these sites are now covered by Interstate 10.

Tanque Verde Ruin (Ariz. BB:14:1) is in the valley of Rincon Creek southeast of Tucson and south of the boundary of Saguaro National Monument. The site is on a low ridge between two washes, and several other similar ruins are located on nearby ridges. Some of the excavated rooms are still visible as shallow depressions. The site was excavated by Emil Haury from 1926 to 1927. Tanque Verde is on private land and has been pothunted on occasion.

The **C. C. Reeve Ruin** (Ariz. BB:11:12) is in Pima County, Arizona, three and one-half miles southeast of the town of Reddington, on the summit of a narrow mesa near the west side of the San Pedro River. This ruin, located on private property, is a thirty-room pueblo constructed of sandstone blocks held by mortar and spalls. The rooms are aligned in house rows. There is a surface ceremonial room with some "kiva" features. Three plazas were found, and a continuous defensive wall encloses the three approachable sides of the site. Each plaza included a ramada area that was walled on three sides and was open to the plaza on the fourth side.

This site is noted for being a prime example of the western Pueblo culture. It has many Pueblo and Salado characteristics in contrast to the pure Hohokam sites in the area. The site was occupied from A.D. 1250 to 1691 and was excavated by Charles C. DiPeso for the Amerind Foundation in 1956.

In the extreme southeast corner of Arizona, two and one-half miles southwest of the ghost town of Gleeson, is the **Gleeson Site** (Ariz FF:5:1). This site sits atop a ridge in the Sulphur Springs Valley near the Dragoon Mountains. Thirty-five houses of six types were excavated here. Some houses were of the Hohokam type, while others were similar to Mogollon dwellings. This site was excavated by the Amerind Foundation under the direction of Carr Tuthill in 1939 to 1940. Today, little evidence remains of the former sub-surface structures. The Gleeson Site was occupied circa A.D. 900.

San Simon Village (Ariz. CC:10:5) is located on the western margin of the San Simon Valley, ten miles west of Bowie, Arizona. It is on the eastern slope of a broad pass leading to the Sulphur Valley about halfway between Dos Cabezas and the southern tip of the Pinolena Mountains. The village consists of sixty-four single excavated house units. These pithouses have lower walls formed by excavation and side entrances. The site also has an interesting ball court. During excavations by E. B. Sayles in 1939 to 1940, the burials uncovered included thirty-eight inhumations and nine cremations. After excavation, the houses were left open and now remain as depressions that give little indication of the original structures. San Simon Village is on private land owned by the Cook Cattle Ranch.

Masonry rooms with original roof beams in cave, Gila Cliff Dwellings National Monument

Entrance to Pueblo Grande Museum, Hohokam figures above door

To the west along the Gila River is one of the westernmost major Hohokam sites. This ruin, northeast of the town of Gila Bend, Arizona, is known as the **Gatlin** or **Gila Bend Site** (Ariz. Z:2:1). It is two and one-half miles north of the junction of Arizona State Routes No. 80 and 84. The site contains twenty-two trash mounds, two ball courts, a crematorium, irrigation canals, and a surrounding pithouse village. There is a platform mound and a possible large house mound, indicating influence from the inhabitants of prehistoric Mexico to the south. This site is on both state and private lands and has been badly damaged by vandals.

A number of other Hohokam sites have been studied in this area. Two of these, **Jackrabbit Village** and **Valshni Village**, are southwest of Tucson on the Papago Indian Reservation. Three sites are located south and east of Tucson. **Paloparado Village** is on the Santa Cruz River north of Nogales, and **Tres Alamos** and **Babocomari Village** are in the valley of the San Pedro River.

Map 8

Prehistoric Ruins of the Upper Verde Valley

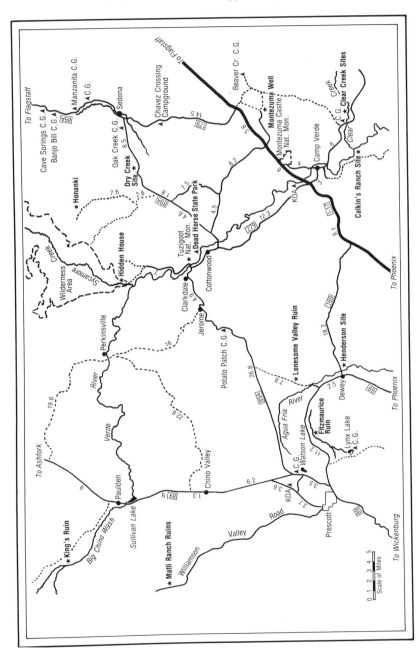

VII

Verde River Area

About one hundred miles north of Phoenix, in the mountains of central Arizona, lies the upper valley of the Verde River, a northern tributary of the Salt River. Prescott, Arizona, an early capital of Arizona Territory, is the major town in this area and is a good place to stay while visiting the ruins. Prescott has two small museums exhibiting artifacts of this and nearby areas. The **Smoki Museum** is open from 10:00 AM to 4:30 PM (except Mondays) from June 1 to September 1. During the remainder of the year, groups may make appointments to see the museum by calling the Prescott Chamber of Commerce at (602) 445-2000. The Smoki Museum is owned and maintained by the Smoki People, a group of Prescott residents who work to preserve the ceremonies and culture of the American Indian. Every August, the Smoki People present their annual ceremonial and snake dance. This spectacular and fascinating event has been presented for fifty-eight years.

The other museum in Prescott is the **Sharlot Hall Museum**, located in the first territorial governor's home on West Gurley Street. It is open from 9:00 AM to 5:00 PM, Tuesday through Saturday, and 1:00 PM to 5:00 PM Sundays. One room in this museum is devoted to Indian artifacts, and there are good exhibits of pottery, baskets, and other artifacts from several prehistoric cultures of Arizona.

Smoki Museum Prescott, Arizona

Prescott's mile-high elevation makes it a pleasant spot to visit in the summer months. The town has several good motels. North of Prescott at Willow Lake is a KOA campground, and several national forest campgrounds are located in the Verde Valley to the east.

The two ruins that are excavated and restored in the Verde Valley and that are therefore recommended to visitors are Tuzigoot National Monument and Montezuma Castle National Monument, with its separate unit at Montezuma Well.

Near Prescott are two well-known excavated ruins—Fitzmaurice Ruin and King's Ruin—and others that are not as well reported. Most of the ruins in this area are classified as Sinagua. This culture is described in Chapter 8. The locations of the ruins are shown on Map #8.

Fitzmaurice Ruin (NA 4031) is approximately six and three-fourths miles east of Prescott on the south bank of Lynx Creek in the Agua Fria drainage. It is located on land owned by the Fain Cattle Company.

This ruin is a twenty-seven-room masonry pueblo measuring sixty-one by fifteen meters. It was probably constructed in three or more phases, as the masonry varies considerably from one section to another. Some of the rooms have no wall openings, and the entrance was probably through a roof hole. Fitzmaurice was occupied from A.D. 1140 to 1300. The original excavations were done in 1933 by Byron Cummings, and in 1974, Franklin Barnett of Prescott did additional excavation.

A site excavated by J. W. Simmons in 1932 was **King's Ruin** (NA 1587), located thirty-five miles north of Prescott on a gravel terrace overlooking the east bank of Chino Creek. It is one mile below the mouth of Walnut Creek. King's Ruin is a pueblo built of mud and boulder walls. It had twelve ground-floor rooms and a second story over part of the structure. A burial area is located east of the pueblo. This ruin was inhabited from approximately A.D. 1000 to 1200. Artifacts and pottery from the Fitzmaurice and King's ruins are exhibited in the Smoki Museum.

Franklin Barnett wrote a novel titled **Crooked Arrow** with its setting in prehistoric times at Fitzmaurice and other nearby ruins. This story gives the reader some idea of what life may have been like in ancient times.

An outstanding ruin in the Verde Valley is **Tuzigoot*** (NA 1261), a word that means "crooked water" in the Apache language. Tuzigoot National Monument is fifty-three miles south of Flagstaff, Arizona, on Arizona Highway No. 89A. It is two miles east of Clarkdale and is the same distance north of the town of Cottonwood. The ruin is situated one-fourth mile from the Verde River on the top and slope of a sharp ridge.

Tuzigoot is a masonry pueblo about 500 by 100 feet and contained 110 rooms. The pueblo was first built on the top of the ridge, and through later construction, it grew down the slopes. It is in an excellent defensive position. There are three smaller outlying room blocks. Eighty-six rooms were excavated, and 411 burials were recovered from the thick trash deposits. This site was excavated by Louis R. Caywood and Edward H. Spicer for the Arizona State Museum in 1933 to 1934. The pueblo had three periods of occupation dating from A.D. 1125, A.D. 1200, and A.D. 1386.

There is a visitors' center with some excellent exhibits and a self-guided trail through the ruin, most of which is accessible to persons who are disabled or in wheelchairs. There is an excellent view of the Verde Valley from the uppermost part of the pueblo. The monument is forty-three acres in size and is open year-round from 8:00 AM to 5:00 PM. The address of the superintendent of Tuzigoot is P.O. Box 68, Clarkdale, Arizona 86324. There are accommodations at Flagstaff and Cottonwood, and campgrounds

Upper section of Tuzigoot National Monument, Arizona

Rooms running down ridge at Tuzigoot National Monument

Excavated rooms of crude Sinagua masonry, metate on floor, Tuzigoot National Monument

are located to the northeast in beautiful Oak Creek Canyon. There are several good Indian arts stores in Sedona on U.S. Highway No. 89A.

Montezuma Castle National Monument* consists of two separate sections, Montezuma Castle and Montezuma Well, seven miles away. Montezuma Castle, the main section, is forty-three miles south of Flagstaff, Arizona, near Interstate 17. It is in a cliff overlooking Beaver Creek, a branch of the Verde River. This ruin is a five-story dwelling of twenty rooms located in an alcove high in the cliff. The rooms were reached by two narrow trails, providing a secure place for the inhabitants. The walls are constructed of limestone blocks laid in mud mortar.

A self-guided walk, known as Sycamore Trail, leads to Montezuma Castle, which cannot be entered because of its fragile condition. Farther on, the trail goes by another ruin called Castle "A." This was a five-story pueblo built at the base of the cliff. It contained about forty-five rooms, some of which can be entered by climbing short ladders. Rangers also conduct tours along Sycamore Trail for groups. There is a visitors' center with exhibits, and most of this monument is accessible to persons in wheelchairs. A picnic ground is located below the visitor's center, along Beaver Creek.

Montezuma Castle National Monument, an easily defended Sinagua structure in the Verde Valley, Arizona

Montezuma Well, Arizona, small masonry rooms below the rim

Small Sinagua structure at Montezuma Well, Montezuma Castle
National Monument, Arizona

The monument is open daily all year from 8:00 AM to 5:00 PM. The
address of the superintendent is the same as that for Tuzigoot.

Montezuma Castle is a Sinagua site inhabited from A.D. 1250
to 1400. It was excavated by Earl Jackson in 1933 to 1934 and was
later stabilized by the National Park Service. Approximately 90
percent of this ruin is original.

Montezuma Well* is seven miles northeast of Montezuma
Castle; directional signs mark the way from Interstate 17. The well
is a huge limestone sink, partially filled with water from an under-
ground spring. Water flows from an outlet at the rate of 1.5 million
gallons per day. The prehistoric Sinagua diverted this water to irrigate their fields. The major ruins in this section are an excavated
pithouse, two small pueblos near the rim, and a few rooms in alcoves below the rim and inside the sink near the outlet. There is a
trail along the rim into the sink and to a cool shady spot at the
outlet. This trail is too steep for most disabled persons. A small
museum and picnic ground are located at the well, and a campground is nearby at Beaver Creek.

Tuzigoot and Montezuma Well and Castle can be visited in
one day and will give the traveler a good introduction to the prehistoric Sinaguas of the Verde Valley.

Another small site, known as **Hidden House,** is seven miles north of Clarkdale in a shallow cave on the east face of Sycamore Canyon. The ruin is above the junction of Sycamore Canyon with the Verde River in Coconino National Forest.

Four masonry rooms in a small cave comprise this site. A burial with many grave goods, including an unusual painted blanket and other perishable goods, was excavated by Clarence R. King in 1934. This site has been dated at A.D. 1150 to 1300. There are a number of similar small sites along the Verde and along the creeks running into it.

Two ruins in the upper Verde River drainage in Loy Canyon are **Honanki Ruin (Bear House)** and **Palatki Ruin (Red House).** These sites are in Prescott National Forest. Little scientific study has been done of these ruins, and they have suffered from vandalization and pothunting over the years.

Palatki consists of two small masonry structures. One section is situated on top of a talus slope against the canyon wall. The front wall was at one time 120 feet long, and much of the single row of rooms had two stories. There is evidence of at least seven ground-floor rooms. The walls are constructed of unshaped red stone slabs laid up in mortar. This pueblo was occupied during Pueblo III times, circa A.D. 1150 to 1250. A few pictographs can be seen on the canyon wall above the ruin.

Honanki was one of the largest ruins in this area. It had approximately thirty ground-floor rooms extending along the base of the cliff for some distance. The long front wall is in ruins, and evidence of the rooms is faint except on the right end of the site. The walls are thicker than those at Palatki but are of similar construction. Parts of Honanki had two or three stories. The first reported survey of these ruins was done in 1895 by Jesse Fewkes.

Of the many small sites in this area, two have been excavated by Franklin Barnett. The **Matli Ranch Ruins** (FB A103) is a group of five small structures ranging from two to ten rooms located on the Matli Ranch, twenty-five miles north-northeast of Prescott on the eastern side of Williamson Valley. Barnett excavated these ruins from 1965 to 1967. Another small site known as **Lonesome Valley Ruin** (NA 11, 139) is east of Prescott in Lonesome Valley, near Arizona Highway No. 209A. This two-room masonry ruin was dug by Barnett in 1971.

Henderson Site is a Hohokam site located near Dewey, Arizona, on the Henderson Ranch east of the Agua Fria River. The site is situated slightly west of a terrace that is one-fourth mile from the river. The site is composed of large Hohokam type pithouses, jacal units, storage bins, and a ramada area. There is an unusual canal running from a spring to an old cistern. Fifteen burials were found; five of these were cremations typical of the Hohokam. The other ten were inhumations indicating influences from the north, where this type of burial is most common. Albert Ward excavated forty-five structures at this Colonial Hohokam site in 1970.

Map 9

Prehistoric Ruins of the Little Colorado River

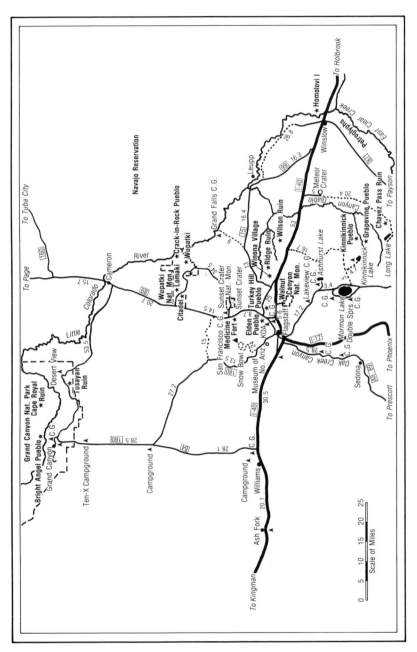

VIII

Little Colorado River Area

This area encompasses the northern or lower portion of the Little Colorado River in the vicinity of Flagstaff, Arizona. It extends roughly from Winslow, Arizona, downstream (north) to the point where the Little Colorado enters the Colorado River, at the east end of Grand Canyon National Park. Flagstaff is the main town in this area and is the home of the **Museum of Northern Arizona,** the leading institution in the study and preservation of the prehistory of the Colorado Plateau. Its publications are of great interest to students of this area, and the H. S. Colton Research Center has an excellent library and research collections. The museum is located a few miles northwest of Flagstaff on Fort Valley Road. It is open 9:00 AM to 5:00 PM, Monday through Saturday, and 1:30 PM to 5:00 PM, Sundays, June through August. The museum telephone number is (602) 774-5211. The museum has a good Indian arts shop and holds annual Hopi and Navajo craftsman shows, where the best work of these tribes is exhibited and offered for sale.

Flagstaff has many motels and is a convenient base from which to visit the numerous ruins to the north and east. Few notable sites are located to the west of Flagstaff. For those who want to camp, there is a large KOA campground in northeastern Flagstaff, or you can stay at Black Bart Campground at Little America off Interstate 40.

Grand Canyon National Park is northwest of Flagstaff and has several ruins open to the public. The campgrounds at Grand Canyon are usually filled during the summer months, and you must register early to get a site. The telephone number is (602) 638-2631.

The Sinagua Culture

Many of the prehistoric settlements in this area and in the Verde Valley exhibit similar traits that have been seen as early Mogollon characteristics by some archeologists. This has caused them to conclude that the Sinagua (which means "without water" in Spanish) is a branch of the Mogollon. However, this conclusion is not accepted by all researchers, some of whom see the Sinagua as a minor culture composed of a combination of traits from the Mogollon, Anasazi, and Hohokam cultures. The Sinagua occupied the area east and southeast of Flagstaff, Arizona, to the vicinity of Winslow, Arizona, and south down into the Verde Valley.

The Sinagua culture had its peak after a geological event that influenced the entire population of this area. This was the eruption of Sunset Crater in A.D. 1065 to 1066. Prior to the eruption, the population of the Flagstaff area was small. The people lived in pithouses located mainly in the higher elevations, where moisture was sufficient. The dry lower portions were very sparsely settled.

The eruption of Sunset Crater covered 800 square miles with volcanic ash and cinders. During or soon after the eruption, most of the inhabitants left this area, but apparently most of them soon returned. Some of the people continued to build pithouses, but soon they began to construct masonry pueblos. The volcanic ash, which at first seemed to decimate the area, actually became the source of a great improvement in agriculture. Where it was laid down in layers of moderate depth, it served as a moisture-retaining mulch, improving productivity. In the area west of Flagstaff, the ash was too deep to permit plant roots to penetrate into the soil, which made this area less productive. This partially accounts for the scarcity of posteruption sites west of Flagstaff. To the east, the wind scattered the ashes in thinner layers down into the lower elevations, which explains the profusion of posteruption settlements to the east and southeast of the crater.

After the eruption, there was a movement of people from the

north, east, and south into the Sinagua country. The evidence for this immigration lies in the new Anasazi, Mogollon, and Hohokam traits present in the area at this time.

The masonry pueblos of the Sinagua show much influence from the Kayenta branch of the Anasazi. These structures were blocks of contiguous rooms, often built of expert masonry, with square, semisubterranean kivas characteristic of the Anasazi. The pottery in these sites also indicates much trade with the Kayenta. Hohokam traits are also evident, in particular the masonry ball court at Wupatki. This is the farthest north that this typical Hohokam structure occurs. There is also a ball court at Winona Village.

Another characteristic of the Sinagua that suggests outside influences are the red types of paddle-and-anvil-made pottery. Two of these plain red types of pottery have been named Sunset Red and Turkey Hill Red. Two of the predominant types of painted pottery are Walnut Black-on-white and Black Mesa Black-on-white, which may have been copies of Anasazi black-on-whites.

The Sinagua culture reached its zenith in the eleventh century. The traits of this culture were a combination of the traits brought in by immigrants from other areas. The burials were both inhumations and cremations. The people used the bow and arrow for hunting. Cultivated food plants included corn, squash, and gourds, and their domesticated animals were dogs and turkeys. They also wove cotton cloth and made baskets. They produced attractive ornaments of stone, shell, and turquoise, including mosaic pendants and lip and nose plugs of red argillite.

Building at Wupatki, one of the major Sinagua sites, ended circa A.D. 1200, and by A.D. 1250 it was abandoned. Nearly all of the inhabitants of the northern Sinagua area had left by A.D. 1300. Although the reason for the exodus is not known, it may have been caused by wind and water erosion that removed much of the ash layer from the area. Some of the population moved south into the Verde Valley, where the Sinagua culture persisted for some time, and others may have traveled farther south to integrate with the Hohokam. It is also believed that some Sinagua may have moved northeast to become the ancestors of a modern Hopi clan. Thus ended another interesting and rich culture of the prehistoric Southwest.

Major Sinagua sites described in this guide are Wupatki, Ridge Ruin, Turkey Hill Pueblo, Elden Pueblo in the Flagstaff area, and Tuzigoot and Montezuma Castle in the Verde Valley. Map #9 shows the locations of prehistoric sites in this area.

Sites of the Little Colorado River Area

Easily accessible from Flagstaff is **Walnut Canyon National Monument*** (NA 739), seven miles east of town on Interstate 40 to the monument entrance, then three miles south to the visitors' center.

Although the ruins at this monument may not be as impressive as others in the area, the beauty of the setting makes it a good place to stop for a few hours to walk the trail and enjoy a picnic. The site includes the remains of over 300 cliff rooms in recesses in the limestone walls of the canyon. These rooms were built by the Sinagua. Surface units, also constructed by the Sinagua, are situated on the mesa top, along with an interesting excavated pithouse of an earlier culture. The population peak in Walnut Canyon was reached in the period A.D. 1100 to 1250, when as many as 600 persons may have resided here. None of the room groups in the canyon are very large.

Row of rooms in recess at Walnut Canyon National Monument near Flagstaff, Arizona

Door and smokehole in wall of Sinagua room, Walnut Canyon
National Monument

Lyn L. Hargrave excavated and stabilized nine rooms with
masonry walls at Walnut Canyon National Monument in 1932.

A three-fourths-mile self-guided walk leads past about twenty-
five of the cliff rooms. Known as Island Trail, it descends 185 feet
into the canyon. Another trail on the mesa top allows visitors to
view several mesa top ruins. There is a visitors' center with a
museum and a picnic ground, but no camping. Wheelchair visitors
can enter the visitors' center and travel the rim trail, but not Island
Trail. Lakeview Campground is nearby. The monument is open
daily from 7:00 AM to 7:00 PM, Memorial Day to Labor Day, and
8:00 AM to 5:00 PM the remainder of the year.

Further southeast of Flagstaff are several large pueblo ruins
that are not well-known. The five that have had at least some excavation and study are Kinnikinnick Pueblo, Grapevine, Pueblo,
Chavez Pass Ruin, and Chevlon Ruin, all south of the Little Colorado, and Homolovi I, north of the river.

Kinnikinnick Pueblo (NA 1629) is located thirty miles southeast of Flagstaff on Anderson Mesa. It is situated on an old lava
flow on the south rim of Kinnikinnick Canyon, about one mile
above its confluence with Grapevine Canyon in Coconino National
Forest.

This ruin is composed of two room blocks of about forty by fifty meters, but now consists of low mounds. The western unit had thirteen rooms, and the eastern unit had sixty rooms. The population is estimated at 100 to 150 persons. The walls were built of sandstone slab masonry, and some portions were two to three stories high. The site is now a large mound of ruined masonry overgrown with brush and cedars. The ruin was occupied from approximately A.D. 1200 to 1350. One room was excavated by the Museum of Northern Arizona under the direction of Milton A. Wetherill, Sydney Conner, and Theodore Stern in 1940. Campgrounds are located at Kinnikinnick and Ashurst lakes in the neighborhood of this ruin.

A nearby site, **Grapevine Pueblo** (NA 2803), is thirty-two miles southeast of Flagstaff and ten miles southeast of Mormon Lake in Coconino National Forest. It is situated on the edge of Grapevine Canyon, immediately south of a seasonal lake on the mesa top.

Grapevine is constructed of crude basalt and sandstone cobble and slab masonry. It contained about sixty ground-floor rooms and possibly several kivas and plazas. The pueblo covers an area twenty by seventy meters and was probably one story in height. An estimated thirty to sixty persons occupied the site during the Pueblo III to Pueblo IV period. Apparently, no scientific excavations have been conducted at Grapevine Pueblo. It now consists of low mounds of building rubble. The general ceramic dates for this late site are A.D. 1300 to 1400.

Approximately twenty miles southwest of Winslow, Arizona, is **Chavez Pass Ruin** (NA 658 and 659). It is located near Chavez Pass and is north of the road through the pass that runs south of Interstate 40 past Meteor Crater to Arizona Highway No. 87. It is situated on a high mesa north of the road in Coconino National Forest.

Chavez Pass Ruin was a large rectangular masonry pueblo built of blocks of lava rock; some low walls are still standing. The site contained 250 or more rooms built in house blocks around courts. It was first excavated by Jesse W. Fewkes in 1896. In 1978 to 1979, excavations by Arizona State University personnel under the direction of Steadman Upham found substantial concentrations of population at the three main room blocks and in the surrounding area from A.D. 1225 to 1375.

Chevlon Ruin (Cakwabaiyaki) (NA 1026) is about six miles southeast of Winslow, Arizona, on Chevlon Creek. It is situated on the top and sides of a prominent gravel ridge on land owned by the state of Arizona.

This ruin contained approximately 300 rooms and had a population of 200 to 400 persons. It was built in three masonry room blocks covering an area of 60 by 100 yards. Parts of the structure were three stories in height, and there are indications of possible kivas. This ruin has been badly damaged by vandals, but some walls still stand. Chevlon was inhabited circa A.D. 1400. It was partially excavated by the Smithsonian Institution under the direction of Jesse W. Fewkes in 1896. There are campgrounds to the south of the ruin at Chevlon Crossing and Chevlon Lake.

Another ruin in this area is **Homolovi I** (NA 952), located about one and one-half miles northeast of Winslow, Arizona. It is on the right bank of the Little Colorado River near the railroad bridge. The site lies on rolling, grass-covered hills on land managed by the U.S. Bureau of Land Management. Other ruins are located along the river to the north.

Homolovi I was a pueblo of approximately 250 rooms covering one and one-half to two acres. It was a two-storied structure of sandstone slab masonry laid up both dry and wet, and there is evidence of a plaza. The population, circa A.D. 1400, is estimated at 150 to 300 persons. Jesse W. Fewkes did some excavation of Homolovi I and other ruins in this area in 1896. Some Hopi legends hold that their ancestors came from Homolovi. Low-standing walls are the chief remains of this pueblo, and in 1979, the Museum of Northern Arizona was conducting investigations here.

Near Winona, Arizona, a small town twenty miles east of Flagstaff, are two well-known ruins of the Sinagua culture. They are named Winona Village and Ridge Ruin.

Winona Village (NA 2133-2135) is one-fourth mile northeast of Winona on a low ridge. Winona was a village of twenty pithouses and five or more surface rooms that may have been storage structures. It was inhabited circa A.D. 1090 and was excavated by the Museum of Northern Arizona under the direction of John C. McGregor in 1935 to 1937. The only remains of this village are holes, backdirt, and scattered cultural debris.

Ridge Ruin (NA 1785) is two and one-half miles east-northeast of Winona, Arizona, in Coconino National Forest. It is situated astride a small ridge overlooking a valley. The ruin consisted of twenty-five rooms, many two stories high. It was built of good masonry similar to that in Chaco Canyon. The site also includes several masonry-lined pithouses near the pueblo and a Hohokam-style ball court 400 feet away.

A very unusual burial was excavated at Ridge Ruin by John McGregor. It contained 600 articles of grave goods. Many were of expert workmanship and artistry. They included 25 pottery vessels, fragments of 8 baskets, 420 arrow points, stone ornaments, 107 turquoise beads and pendants, and thousands of stone beads. It is concluded that this was the burial of a man of high status, perhaps a chief or medicine man of the ancient Sinagua inhabitants.

This Sinagua site was inhabited from A.D. 1085 to 1207 and was excavated by McGregor in 1939. Presently, only a few low-standing walls remain.

Twenty-six miles east of Flagstaff and one and one-half miles east of Padre Canyon is **Wilson Ruin** (NA 1139). It was a six-room masonry pueblo with an earlier, underlying brush structure. Wilson Ruin was inhabited from A.D. 1150 to 1200 by people of the Sinagua culture and was excavated by Lyn L. Hargrave in 1930. The site presently consists of walls, a mound, and scattered cultural materials.

Elden Pueblo (NA 142) is in a pine forest seven miles northeast of Flagstaff, Arizona. It is situated on a ridge between Elden Mountain and Sheep Hill in Coconino National Forest. Elden is a masonry pueblo of one and two stories and contained over sixty-five rooms. Situated around the main building were three small, one-story houses of three to five rooms. There was also one large, ground-level kiva at this site.

Elden Pueblo was occupied from A.D. 1120 to 1220. Jesse Fewkes did the first excavation here in 1926. He dug 150 burials and recovered many grave goods. Later excavation and stabilization were done by the Museum of Northern Arizona and the National Forest Service. Some walls still stand at this site, which makes it interesting to view.

Turkey Hill Pueblo (NA 660) is at the base of Turkey Hill, three miles northeast of Flagstaff in Coconino National Forest. It is a masonry pueblo of at least thirty rooms. Three small units of two to four rooms lie to the southeast of the main building. There are permanent metates in a lava flow to the north of the pueblo. Turkey Hill Pueblo was occupied circa A.D. 1100 to 1300 and was excavated by Byron Cummings in 1927 to 1928. The present remains of this ruin consist of low-standing walls and scattered cultural debris.

The most extensive and well-preserved ruins in the northern

Little Colorado area are those in **Wupatki National Monument.**[*]
An estimated eight hundred ruins lie within the monument's fifty-six square miles. Most of the ruins are of the posteruption Sinagua culture, but pre-eruption pithouses have also been found under the layer of volcanic ash deposited by the eruption of Sunset Crater. Visitors to this area are advised to spend a day or two at Wupatki. The address of Wupatki National Monument is Tuba Star Route, Flagstaff, Arizona 86003. The telephone number is (602) 774-7000.

The monument entrance is thirty miles north of Flagstaff on U.S. Highway No. 89. The visitors' center and **Wupatki Ruin** (NA

Wall of sandstone and basalt blocks, Nalakihu Ruin, Wupatki National Monument

405) are fourteen miles from the entrance. Three major ruins are located along the entrance road. These are **Lomaki**[*] (NA 379), **Nalakihu**[*] (NA 358), and **Citadel Ruin**[*] (NA 355). Lomaki, a short distance north of the entrance road, is a partially excavated pueblo ruin on the edge of a wash. The one tree-ring date from this site is A.D. 1192. It is worth the short hike to see this site and contemplate what this country must have looked like after the eruption of Sunset Crater to the south.

Nalakihu and Citadel are located south of the road a short distance beyond Lomaki. Booklets for a self-guided trail are available at the small parking lot. Nalakihu, which means "long house" in Hopi, is a small pueblo of ten ground-floor and several second-story rooms. It is built of sandstone and lava block masonry. Dale King did some excavation at Nalakihu in 1932. This ruin is at the base of a lava hill close to the parking lot. The trail leads up the hill to the top where the Citadel Ruin is situated. The Citadel has not been excavated, but it had an estimated thirty rooms and a population of fifty to sixty persons. The location of this ruin suggests a need for defense on the part of those Sinagua people who built it.

Wupatki Pueblo, a Sinagua site north of Flagstaff, Arizona

From Citadel Ruin, several other sites can be seen on nearby mesas, and a large limestone sink is immediately to the south. The pottery found at Nalakihu and Citadel ruins indicates that the inhabitants of these adjacent sites had different origins prior to their move to this area. Nalakihu and Wukoki are accessible to persons in wheelchairs. Wukoki* is located three miles northeast of Wupatki on an unpaved road.

Nine miles further along the entrance road is the visitors' center and the main ruin, **Wupatki*** (NA 405), meaning "tall house" in Hopi. This ruin contained approximately two hundred

SUE+GAYL @WUKOKI 9:00am SUN 29 May 88

Large circular, unroofed ceremonial structure, Wupatki National Monument, Arizona

Wupatki Pueblo, large boulder incorporated in masonry wall with wooden support underneath

SAW PETROGLYPHS @ LOMAKI (& RUINS BY BOX CANYON) - SEE p.101

rooms of all types and housed an estimated two hundred persons. The outstanding feature of this site is a ball court of the type common at Hohokam sites far to the south. This indicates immigration from the south after the A.D. 1065 eruption of Sunset Crater. There is also a large, circular, unroofed amphitheater that may have served as a ceremonial structure. Wupatki shows the influences of Anasazi, Hohokam, and Mogollon people, who moved into this area in posteruption times. Wupatki Ruin was excavated by the Museum of Northern Arizona and the National Park Service in 1933 to 1934, 1941 to 1942, 1952 to 1953, and 1965.

There is a small museum at the visitors' center and a self-guided trail through Wupatki, much of which is accessible to handicapped persons. The monument is open from 8:00 AM to 7:00 PM, May to September, and 8:00 AM to 5:00 PM the rest of the year. A picnic ground is located along the entrance road. No camping is available at Wupatki, but there is a good campground beyond the visitors' center at Sunset Crater National Monument.

Three miles northeast of Flagstaff in Medicine Valley is an unusual ruin known as **Medicine Fort** (NA 862), located in Coconino National Forest. This is a site from the time prior to the eruption of Sunset Crater. Masonry walls four feet thick and eight feet

Medicine Fort north of Flagstaff, thick walls on right surround an open plaza *(Museum of Northern Arizona photo)*

high surround a court or compound that is twenty-eight feet by fifty-six feet; some of these walls are still standing. Along one side is a row of small rooms used as granaries. Possibly this ruin was a defensive site, but it is unlike any other known structure. Medicine Fort was built in A.D. 1061 and excavated in 1930 by Lyn Hargrave.

Several prehistoric sites are located in **Grand Canyon National Park**, a few of which have been excavated and restored. **Tusayan Ruin*** (Echo Cliffs 13:1 GP) is located at the Wayside Museum of Archeology, twenty miles east of Grand Canyon Village on Arizona Highway No. 64, near Lipan Point.

Tusayan Ruin is a thirty-room, two-story masonry pueblo built in the shape of a "U." It is constructed of limestone boulders laid in mortar. The structures include eight living rooms, storage rooms, and two kivas. The dates for this pueblo are A.D. 1170 to 1205. It was excavated by Emil Haury in 1930. This site also includes an excavated, circular pithouse, circa A.D. 800. Tusayan Ruin is open all year, and there are guided tours during the summer months.

On the north rim, on Walhalla Plateau, southeast of Kaibab, Arizona, is **Cape Royal Ruin*** (GC 212). It has been excavated and is open to the public. Cape Royal is a few miles back from the cape itself and was excavated by Douglas Schwartz.

In the bottom of the Grand Canyon near the Colorado River is **Bright Angel Pueblo*** (NA 5602). This ruin was first mentioned in 1869 by John Wesley Powell, who led the first expedition down the Colorado River. In 1969, in celebration of the centennial of Powell's visit, the site was excavated and stabilized by Schwartz for the School of American Research.

The pueblo is located east of the confluence of Bright Angel Creek and the Colorado River and is forty yards west of the Kaibab suspension bridge. It is situated at the top of a talus slope thirty feet above the river level. The Kaibab Trail crosses the talus slope immediately above the pueblo.

This seven-room pueblo was built in two phases. The first structure was a single rectangular room that was occupied from A.D. 1050 to 1060. Five rooms and a rectangular kiva were built in the second phase and were occupied from A.D. 1100 to 1140. The pueblo is constructed of unshaped horizontal blocks of schist laid up in a sandy mortar. Five of the living rooms have a central fire pit. The features of the kiva include a central fire pit, a ventilator, and possibly a deflector. This ruin has been stabilized and is easily accessible from Kaibab Trail.

Upstream from Kaibab suspension bridge and eighty feet above the river is a small masonry granary. It is located in a cleft in the north face of inner Granite Gorge. The construction and location of this granary indicate that it was probably used by the inhabitants of Bright Angel Pueblo.

In order to visit Bright Angel Pueblo, it is necessary to hike or ride muleback into the mile-deep canyon. Reservations for a mule trip must be made at least one day in advance. It is possible to hike in and out of the Grand Canyon in one day, but it is a strenuous trip. It is best for most persons to camp overnight or stay at Phantom Valley Ranch in the canyon. Reservations are necessary for lodging in Phantom Valley. Hikers in the canyon should use special caution. The steep trails and heat of summer can turn a short hike into a very tiring and potentially dangerous experience.

Low wall surrounds an oval ball court showing Hohokam influence at Wupatki Pueblo

Room at Wupatki showing crude masonry and niches in walls of this Sinagua pueblo

Map 10

Prehistoric Ruins of the Upper Little Colorado River

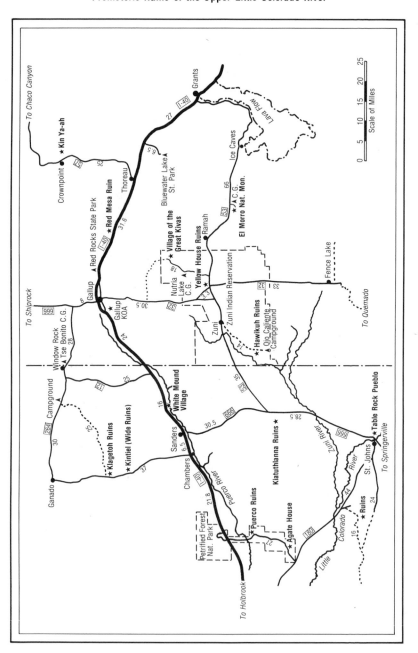

IX

Upper Little Colorado River Area

This area includes the upper tributaries of the Little Colorado River in northeastern Arizona and northwestern New Mexico. One of the major branches is the Rio Puerco of the West, which has its source near the Arizona–New Mexico border and flows in a southwesterly direction to join the Little Colorado near Holbrook, Arizona. The Little Colorado heads in western New Mexico and flows in a northwest direction by St. Johns, Arizona, where it is joined by the Zuni River.

This area extends from Gallup, New Mexico, to St. Johns, Arizona, in the southwest and from El Morro National Monument on the east to Petrified National Forest on the west. It is a country of dry washes and sparse, grass-covered hills with some trees along the water courses and in the higher elevations to the east.

A number of ruins are located in this area, but very few have been restored. Most of the excavations have been backfilled, and little evidence remains of the prehistoric structures. Map #10 contains the locations of the prehistoric sites described in this section. The prehistoric inhabitants of this area were Anasazi with some Mogollon influences from the south.

The only town of any size within this area is Gallup, New Mexico, on Interstate 40. The Museum of Indian Arts in Gallup is definitely worth a few hours' visit. It is located at 103 West Sixty-Sixth Avenue and is open from 9:00 AM to noon and 1:00 PM to

5:00 PM, Monday through Friday, and 9:00 AM to noon on Saturdays.

Red Rocks State Park, five minutes east of Gallup on Interstate 40, is one of the better places to camp in this area. Each year in September, the Inter Tribal Indian Ceremonial is held in Gallup. This celebration draws a large crowd of tourists with all of the attendant problems and has been criticized by some American Indian groups as an exploitation of the Indian. In spite of these problems, it does provide a good variety of Indian arts and crafts for those who want to view or buy, and the festivities include Indian dances and a rodeo. Recently, the ceremonial has been held at Red Rocks State Park. The address and telephone number at Red Rocks is P.O. Box 328, Church Rock, New Mexico 87311; (505) 722–5564.

Northwest of Gallup is Window Rock, capital of the Navajo nation. The Navajo Tribal Museum and Arts and Crafts Guild are located here. There is a campground and the Navajo-owned Window Rock Motor Inn for the traveler staying in this small community.

Two excavated and partially restored ruins are located in Petrified Forest National Park*: **Agate House** and **Puerco Ruins**. No campground is available at this park, so these ruins must be viewed on a drive through the area.

The prehistoric and historic Indian ruins on the Zuni Indian Reservation, south of Gallup, can be visited by camping on the reservation or at El Morro National Monument to the east. The El Morro campground is attractive and usually is not crowded. There are no restored ruins on the Zuni Reservation, but the Zuni tribe is supporting some archeological work.

Yellowhouse Ruin* (LA 493), near the junction of New Mexico Highways No. 53 and No. 32 north of the Rio Pescado, is evidenced by an overgrown mound and remains of low walls. The Zuni tribe is encouraging tourists and has primitive campgrounds at Blackrock, Nutria Lakes, Ojo Caliente, and Eustace Lake, with minimal facilities. Visitors may fish and hunt on the Zuni Reservation if they purchase permits from the tribe. This reservation is a good spot to visit for those who like out-of-the-way places without crowds. The Zuni make fine silver jewelry inlaid with turquoise and other stones.

In the northern part of this area, the Navajo weavers make fine rugs. The rug-weaving areas of Ganado, Wide Ruins, Pine Springs, and Burntwater are the source of many excellent rugs featuring the beautiful muted colors produced by vegetal dyes. They are rather expensive but in the long run are worth the cost. Rug auctions are held at the small village of Crownpoint, New Mexico, south of Chaco Canyon, several times a year.

Near Wide Ruins Trading Post, eighteen miles north of Chambers, Arizona, on Arizona Highway No. 63, is **Kin Tiel,** or "Wide Ruins" (NA 1015). It is on the Navajo Indian Reservation and is situated on either side of a small wash that is an eastern tributary of Wide Ruin wash. Directions may be obtained at Wide Ruins Trading Post.

This Anasazi ruin is a large masonry pueblo built in the shape of an oval or butterfly. The pueblo consisted of 150 to 200 rooms covering an area of 550 feet by 300 feet. It contained several kivas. The dates from kiva no. 1 are A.D. 1226 to 1276. Kin Tiel was partially excavated by Jesse W. Fewkes in 1897 and again by Lyn Hargrave in 1929. There is a campground to the northeast at Antelope Lake.

Petrified Forest National Park is twenty miles southeast of Holbrook, Arizona. From the west, it is best to go southeast on U.S. Highway No. 180 to the southern entrance, then through the park to the northern entrance on Interstate 40. Traveling east, you should reverse this route.

This park is noted for the great numbers of beautiful petrified trees and a portion of the colorful Painted Desert. There are two excavated and partially restored ruins in this park. **Puerco Ruin*** (NA 875) is located eleven miles from the north entrance near the Puerco River ranger station. **Agate House*** is a short distance north of the southern, or Rainbow Forest, entrance. Puerco Ruin is a rectangular masonry ruin of 150 rooms. It was occupied circa A.D. 1300. There are information signs at the ruin and an excellent view of the Puerco River valley. Agate House is a small, partially restored pueblo situated on top of a ridge. This ruin is very colorful because it was built of blocks of multicolored petrified wood.

Stone Axe Ruin (NA 1020) is 2.8 miles southeast of Agate Bridge. It is situated on the middle of three small ridges. Stone Axe was a one-story pueblo of 200 rooms covering an area of 150 by 200 meters. It was built of sandstone slab masonry. This ruin was occupied circa A.D. 1300 to 1400 and was excavated by Walter Hough in 1901.

Two other ruins in Petrified Forest National Park are **Flattop Site** and **Twin Buttes Site.** The former is a pithouse village of twenty-five houses in the southern part of the park, northeast of park headquarters and one mile southeast of the road. Twin Buttes is southeast of Agate House, one mile east of the road near Dry Creek. It is situated along the base of a sandstone escarpment.

The petrified wood and desert colors are the main attractions at Petrified Forest, and relatively little attention has been given to the prehistoric remains in the park. Visitors should be careful not to remove any petrified wood or other natural objects from the park. Specimens can be purchased at park headquarters, and you can look for pieces on private land *with permission* of the landowners.

Unfortunately, there are no camping facilities in Petrified Forest National Park, and none close by. Campers may stay at the Holbrook KOA or at campgrounds northeast along Interstate 40.

Twenty miles north of St. Johns, Arizona, is **Kiatuthlanna Ruins** (LA 553). The ruins are one mile north of the Twin Salt Lakes on the old Long H Ranch. This site consists of eighteen pithouses and a pueblo ruin of forty-nine rooms, four kivas, and the vestiges of three jacal pole-and-mud structures. The pueblo is a compact "L"-shaped building made of stone, adobe, and veneered walls. Kiatuthlanna was excavated by Frank H. H. Roberts in 1929. The site had two occupations, one in early Pueblo I times and a later one in the early Pueblo III period.

Table Rock Pueblo is one mile east of St. Johns. It is about 500 feet east of the Little Colorado River on the Davis Ranch. The ruin is situated on a very low rock outcropping between two hills. Table Rock is a one-story pueblo of sixty to one hundred rooms arranged in two rows, each three rooms wide. There are two rectangular kivas at this site. The population has been estimated at 100 to 125 persons. Table Rock was inhabited circa A.D. 1375. In 1958, Paul Martin of the Field Museum of Natural History excavated fifty rooms and two kivas. As with most of the ruins in this area, Table Rock now consists of a low mound.

Allantown Ruins are three and one-half miles south of the small Arizona settlement of the same name. The site is south of the Puerco River and west of Whitewater Creek. Allantown is a large, multicomponent site with two groups of pithouses. A small masonry pueblo with a circular kiva is situated at the foot of a talus slope below the main portion of the site. Another similar pueblo is located one mile upstream. The pithouses were occupied A.D. 844 to 853 and the pueblo A.D. 1002 to 1016. This site was excavated by Frank H. H. Roberts in 1931 to 1933.

On a hilltop overlooking the Puerco River is **White Mound Village.** It is north of the river, two miles east of Houck, Arizona. White Mound is a village of six pithouses, three blocks of surface masonry storerooms, and associated hearths and storage cists. The pithouses were from ten to fifteen square meters in area, and the pole-and-mud roofs were supported by four posts. This Anasazi site was occupied A.D. 783 to 803.

A number of ruins are located on the Zuni Indian Reservation thirty miles south of Gallup. **Hawikuh Ruin** (LA 37) is the best known. Permission to visit these sites may be obtained from tribal headquarters in Zuni. This was probably one of the first pueblos seen by the Spanish in 1540. Hawikuh is fifteen miles southwest of modern Zuni Pueblo and a few miles northwest of the tiny village of Ojo Caliente. To reach it, go north of Ojo Caliente about two miles, and take a dirt road to the west. Proceed two miles on this road to where it goes over the end of a low ridge. The ruin on the left runs along the ridge, which is two and one-half miles east of the Zuni River. There is an older site about one mile northeast along this same ridge.

Hawikuh consists of five groups of rooms and a Spanish mission church covering approximately three acres. There was an estimated total of 1,060 rooms. The room groups were formed of solidly massed rooms of from one to three stories. This site was extensively excavated by Frederick W. Hodge in 1917 to 1923, but the final report was not published until 1966. The ruin was occupied circa A.D. 1381 to 1480. There is a small campground at Ojo Caliente Lake south of the village. Visitors to Zuni should be careful of driving on unpaved roads during or shortly after the infrequent rains.

In the northern part of the Zuni Reservation is the site known as the **Village of the Great Kivas** (LA 631). It is seventeen miles northeast of Zuni Pueblo on Zuni No. 5, near Nutria Village, and is situated on the talus at the foot of low cliffs.

This site has three pueblos, the largest of which has sixty-four rooms and two great kivas similar to those in Chaco Canyon to the northeast. This site was excavated by Frank H. H. Roberts in 1930. It was inhabited circa A.D. 1031. At the nearby Nutria Lakes are two campgrounds with pit toilets and tables but no drinking water. Visitors may fish for trout in the lakes providing they have a Zuni tribal permit.

Thirty-five miles east of Zuni Pueblo on New Mexico Highway No. 53 is **El Morro National Monument.** * From Grants, New Mexico, it is forty-two miles south on New Mexico Highway No. 53. The address of the monument is Ramah, New Mexico 87321.

There are two pueblo ruins on top of El Morro Rock. One,

On top of this 200 foot high mesa-point sits Atsinna Pueblo, El Morro National Monument

named **Atsinna,** is 200 feet by 300 feet in size, and it had a heavy outer wall. Part of this pueblo was three stories in height. The site also includes two kivas, one circular and the other square, and three reservoir depressions. The trail to the top of the rock passes the many prehistoric, Spanish, and English inscriptions for which El Morro is noted. At the base of the rock is a natural basin that collects runoff. This has been a reliable source of water for centuries. Wheelchair occupants can enter the visitors' center and can see many of the inscriptions by use of a bypass around the visitors' center, but cannot tour the pueblos on top of the rock.

Atsinna was occupied from approximately A.D. 1100 to 1200 and was excavated by Richard B. Woodbury in 1954 to 1955. There is a visitors' center and small museum at El Morro and a nice small campground. The address here is c/o Navajo Lands Group, P.O. Box 539, Farmington, New Mexico 87401.

South of El Morro and thirteen miles north of Quemado, New Mexico, is **Sandstone Hill Pueblo Ruin** (NA 11,233); it is located on private property. The ruin is about one-half mile east of the road and fifty yards south-southeast from the base of a rugged hill for which the ruin is named.

This is a ruin of the Cibola branch of the Anasazi culture. It is an eighteen-room masonry-walled pueblo with an exterior cooking area. The ruin was excavated by Franklin Barnett in 1971, and it was determined that Sandstone Hill Pueblo was occupied A.D. 1115 to 1300.

East of Gallup, New Mexico, at the head of Red Mesa Valley near Coolidge, New Mexico, is **Red Mesa Ruin.** It is a six-room house that varies considerably in construction from room to room. Fire pits are located outside the rooms. A pithouse twelve feet in diameter and located twenty feet from the house may have been used for ceremonial purposes. Red Mesa Ruin was occupied A.D. 875 to 916 and was excavated by Emil Haury in the late 1920s.

Twenty-three miles north of Chambers, Arizona, on the Navajo Reservation, is Klagetoh Trading Post. Near the trading post are the **Klagetoh Ruins** (NA 1016). It is a large masonry surface pueblo. The one tree-ring date from this pueblo is A.D. 1112.

Bidahochi Ruin (NA 1054, LA 513) is about thirty-four miles southeast of Keams Canyon on Arizona Highway No. 77. It is on the east side of Tesbito wash, an upper branch of Cottonwood wash near Indian Wells on the Navajo Indian Reservation.

Map 11

Prehistoric Ruins of the Hopi Mesas and Canyon de Chelly

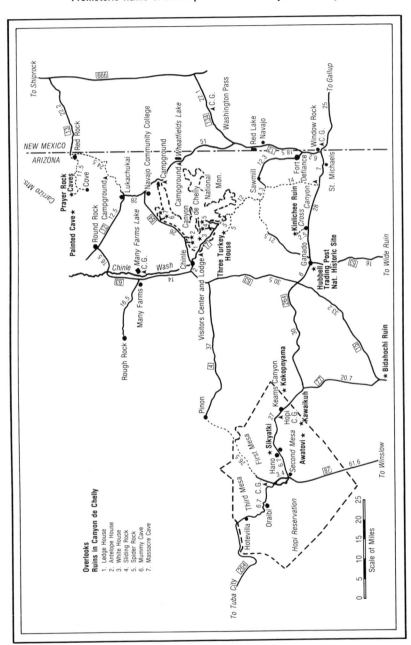

Overlooks
Ruins in Canyon de Chelly
1. Ledge House
2. Antelope House
3. White House
4. Sliding Rock
5. Spider Rock
6. Mummy Cave
7. Massacre Cave

Scale of Miles

0 5 10 15 20 25

X

The Hopi and Canyon de Chelly Area

This area extends from the Hopi mesas in northeastern Arizona to Canyon de Chelly National Monument near the Arizona–New Mexico border. Except for that portion on the Hopi Reservation, it is entirely on the huge Navajo Indian Reservation. Locations of the ruins and other features in this area are shown on Map #11.

The contemporary Hopi pueblos are located on, or near, the three mesas that extend southward from Black Mesa. The only accommodation near Hopi country is the Hopi-owned motel on Second Mesa. Campers can stay at the campground on Second Mesa or at the more attractive campground at Keams Canyon east of First Mesa. (The three Hopi mesas are named First Mesa, Second Mesa, and Third Mesa, from east to west.)

In spite of its out-of-the-way location, the area of the Hopi mesas is a good place to visit for persons interested in the prehistoric cultures and contemporary Indians of the Southwest. The Hopis have been influenced less by European and American cultures than any other Indian tribe. Therefore, their culture, and particularly their dwellings, are the most similar to those of their prehistoric ancestors. The pueblo of Old Oraibi has been inhabited for perhaps 1,000 years, and life for some of the more traditional Hopis has not changed a great deal. The arts and crafts of the Hopis, especially their jewelry, kachinas, and pottery, are some of the finest in the Southwest. The Hopi Arts and Crafts Guild on Second Mesa and McGee's Trading Post at Keams Canyon have good selections, and at times items may be purchased from the makers at their homes. The Hopi ceremonials, especially the Snake Dance, are some of the most impressive in the United States. Permission should be sought from the Hopis to observe any of their ceremonies or to take pictures of the people of the dwellings. This should also be strictly adhered to at all pueblos or Indian villages.

The major ruins in the Hopi area include: Awatovi, Kawaikuh, Sityatki, and Kokopnyama. It is liable to be hot in this country in the summer, and it is usually dry. Persons leaving paved roads should take plenty of water and, if it begins to rain, get back to the pavement as soon as possible. Flash floods in this area can make dirt roads impassable in a few minutes. I do not intend to discourage anyone from visiting Hopiland, but it may be somewhat of an adventure, and it is not the place for people who want fancy accommodations and a luxury vacation. It should also be noted that no liquor is sold on the Hopi or surrounding Navajo reservations. In spite of the vandalism of some Hopi ruins and shrines and disrespect for their homes, persons who do respect their property and customs will find them a friendly and hospitable people.

Awatovi Ruins (NA 820) are located on the Hopi Reservation south of Keams Canyon. The ruins are situated on the edge of Antelope Mesa above Jeddito wash.

Awatovi is a large sandstone pueblo ruin covering twenty-three acres. The western portion of the ruin, known as the Western Mound, was the first part built and occupied. The site also includes ruins of a Spanish mission consisting of three churches, a friary, and a barracks-stable that were built in A.D. 1630. Awatovi was partially excavated by J. O. Brew from 1935 to 1939. Over 1,300 rooms and kivas were dug, and a great deal of pottery and artifacts were found. A book by Watson Smith, *Painted Pottery of the Western Mound*, gives an excellent description and illustrations of the beautiful yellow wares found here. Awatovi was inhabited from A.D. 1630 to 1700, but in 1700, Hopis from nearby pueblos attacked and burned it. These tribesmen were dismayed over the Spanish residency at Awatovi and the acceptance of Spanish culture and religion by the Awatovians. This site has been backfilled, and little remains except the large mounds and a great deal of broken pottery.

118

About four miles northeast of Awatovi is the ruin known as **Kawaikuh (Kawaik-a)** (NA 1001). It is located on the southeast edge of Antelope Mesa between two gorges. This is a very large Pueblo III to IV masonry pueblo. The ruin is of irregular arrangement with courts enclosed by large and small room blocks. It was occupied from A.D. 1350 to 1649. The site was excavated by Walter Hough in the early 1900s. Today it is a low mound with a few faint remains of walls.

The third ruin to be included in this area is **Sikyatki Pueblo** (NA 814). It is in Upper Polacca wash near the Hopi village of Walpi. The ruin lies in the foothills a few hundred yards from the base of a mesa that is about three miles east of the settlement of Coyote Spring. The pueblo was rectangular in shape and had an enclosed plaza. Two large house clusters are connected by a narrow row of rooms. The peak population has been estimated at three hundred to four hundred persons. The site, excavated by Jesse Fewkes in 1895, is noted for the excellent pottery known as Sikyatki Polychrome. During Fewkes' work, examples of this fine ware inspired the famous Hopi potter, Nampeyo, to initiate a revival of Hopi pottery making, which continues today.

Kokopnyama (NA 1019), also known as **Cottonwood Ruin,** is one mile northeast of Jeddito Trading Post on the north side of Jeddito Valley. It is five miles southeast of Keams Canyon and runs along the edge of Antelope Mesa for 600 feet. This was a large two-story pueblo of several hundred rooms built of poor-quality masonry. It covers an area of ten to twelve acres. The site includes two to five plazas and seven large kivas. It was occupied from approximately A.D. 1275 to 1380 and was excavated by Lyn Hargrave in 1929.

Other large pueblo ruins in the Hopi area are: **Chakpahu, Nesuftanga, Lululongturque, Hoyapi Pueblo** (NA 837), and **Pociolelena** (Whistling Quail Pueblo) (NA 1603).

Canyon de Chelly National Monument* is sixty-five miles northeast of Keams Canyon via Arizona Highways No. 264 and No. 63, on good paved roads to Chinle, Arizona, then two miles east to monument headquarters.

Hiking or driving alone in the canyons is prohibited in order to protect the ancient ruins and the privacy of the Navajos who reside there during the summer months. The best way to see the prehistoric ruins and the beautiful red rock canyons is to take a whole day or a half-day guided tour in four-wheel drive trucks. These

Navajo farm and hogan (house) near trail to White House Ruin in Canyon de Chelly

Navajo fields in bottom of Canyon del Muerto, Canyon de Chelly National Monument, Arizona

trips may be arranged at Thunderbird Lodge east of Chinle, Arizona, from May to November. Owners of four-wheel drive vehicles may hire an approved Navajo guide to accompany them into the canyons. Visitors may find lodging at Thunderbird Lodge or at several motels in the nearby town of Chinle, where all services and supplies are available. The address of Thunderbird Lodge is Box 548, Chinle, Arizona 86503; telephone (602) 674-5443. Cottonwood Campground is situated in a shady cottonwood grove in the valley below the visitors' center. This campground has flush toilets, wash facilities, drinking water, and a disposal station, but no hookups.

The visitors' center has a small museum that displays artifacts from the sites in the national monument, and a Navajo hogan is exhibited on the grounds. The Thunderbird Lodge facilities and the visitors' center are accessible to persons in wheelchairs. Disabled persons who are able to take a rather rough ride could take a four-wheel drive tour of the canyons. Some of the canyon overlooks are accessible to wheelchair persons, others are not.

There are paved roads near the north and south rims of the canyons with short turnoffs to overlook points above some of the ruins. Photographs of the ruins and the canyons can be taken from these overlooks; a telephoto lens is very useful to obtain better pictures of the distant ruins. From White House Trail Overlook, on the South Rim Drive, a steep trail leads down into the canyon and across the canyon floor to White House Ruin. This hike takes about three hours and may be impassable during the spring runoff. There are also interesting ranger-guided hikes to view the ruins and petroglyphs in the lower portion of the canyon. These excursions involve hiking down into the canyon at Tsegi Overlook, then through the canyon to its mouth. Horses may be rented at the stables near Thunderbird Lodge for guided rides into the canyon. During the summer months, Navajo families live in the canyons, and the privacy of their homes and fields should be respected.

Along the South Rim Drive, the following ruins may be seen from the overlooks: First Ruin (CDC-47), Junction Ruin, White House Ruin (CDC-75), and Sliding Rock Ruin (CDC-107). There is also an overlook near the junction of Canyon de Chelly and Monument Canyon, from which Spider Rock can be seen. Spider Rock is a thin sandstone spire towering 800 feet over the canyon floor. The overlooks accessible from the North Rim Drive provide distant views of Ledge Ruin (CDM-2), Antelope House (CDM-10),

Mummy Cave (Tse'-ya-kin) (CDM-174), Yucca Cave, and Massacre Cave (CDM-176).

The four-wheel drive tours usually go up the main canyon, then turn right up Canyon de Chelly to the ruins. They then backtrack and take the left fork up Canyon del Muerto, where most of the major ruins are seen. These tours stop at only a few of the many sites.

A number of large petroglyph sites can be seen in the lower part of the main canyon; two of these are known as **The Wall** (**Newspaper Rock**) (CDC-16) and **Petroglyph Rock** (CDC-139), a 100-foot monolith near the mouth of Cottonwood Canyon. In the main canyon, the first major ruin seen is appropriately named **First Ruin** (CDC-47). This large Pueblo III structure was built by Mesa Verde people who moved south into this area. About twelve rooms and two kivas were constructed during the Mesa Verde occupation. This ruin is seventy-five feet above the canyon floor and was reached by a hand-and-toe trail in the rock. The petroglyphs at this site consist of human figures, handprints, and geometric forms in white, red, and gray.

Farther up Canyon de Chelly on the left side is **White House Ruin** (NA 2187), the best known of the estimated four hundred

White House Ruin in Canyon de Chelly

Lower section of White House Ruin, Canyon de Chelly National Monument, Navajo Indian Reservation

White House Ruin, petroglyph of human on cliff face between upper and lower sections

ruins in the monument. This site is now divided into two sections, one on the canyon floor at the base of the canyon wall, and the other directly above it in a cave. These two sections were once joined by the four-story lower building. The lower section had approximately sixty rooms and four kivas, and the small upper section had ten rooms. White House housed an estimated thirty to forty persons. The major portion was built by Mesa Verde people during the Pueblo III period; it was occupied from A.D. 1251 to 1284. This ruin was named for the covering of white gypsum clay on the facade of the upper section. There is a petroglyph of a human figure with upraised arms on the cliff above the lower ruin.

Earl H. Morris conducted some of the most extensive excavations in these canyons from 1923 to 1932; in recent years, the National Park Service has done some excavation and stabilization of the ruins.

Tse'-ta's Ruin (CDC 76 & 77) is a few miles upstream from White House. Excavated by Charlie Steen in 1966, it was the first ruin in the monument to be excavated with modern scientific methods. The site was occupied from Basketmaker to Pueblo III times. The Pueblo II structures are in two sections; the larger northern section had fourteen rooms and four kivas, and the smaller southern section had eight rooms and one kiva. Parts of the structure were three stories high.

Another large ruin on the left-hand side of the canyon as you proceed upstream is known as **Sliding Rock Ruin** (CDC-107). It can be seen from an overlook on the South Rim Drive. This Pueblo III ruin is also divided into two sections. The total number of rooms in both sections was thirty-five to fifty. Four kivas were also found. This ruin is situated on a sloping ledge 150 feet above the canyon floor. It was reached by a hand-and-toe hole trail. The site also has some petroglyphs of a flute player, handprints, and birds.

Proceeding up Canyon del Muerto, the first stop of most tours is made at **Antelope House** (CDM-10). This ruin is five miles above the junction of Canyon del Muerto and Canyon de Chelly. This large ruin is situated on the valley floor against the foot of the cliff. Although erosion from flooding has taken its toll on Antelope House, some walls are still four stories in height. This ruin contained forty to fifty rooms and four kivas. Parts of this site have been excavated and stabilized, making it a good place to visit and photograph. This Pueblo III ruin is named for the figures of four antelope painted by a Navajo on the cliff twenty-five feet above the canyon floor. Across the canyon from Antelope House is the noted

Tomb of the Weaver. This is the grave of an old man who was wrapped in two very fine blankets, one of eagle feathers and the other of white cotton. The rich grave goods, weaving tools, and large skeins of cotton yarn indicate that this man may have been a highly honored weaver.

Under a large overhang upstream from Antelope House is the site known as **Standing Cow Ruin** (CDM-4). This ruin is named for the large figure of a blue-headed cow painted by a Navajo on the cliff above the ruin. This is one of the largest ruins in the canyon. It covered an area of 400 by 40 feet and contained at least sixty rooms and three kivas. However, very little remains today. A stone Navajo hogan and sheep corrals are also located at this site. The petroglyphs in this area include prehistoric drawings of human figures, a hunchbacked archer, and several types of animals.

Farther up the canyon is **Big Cave** (Tse-ya-tso) (CDM-155), a very large Basketmaker site. The tree-ring dates from this site range from A.D. 331 to A.D. 835, indicating that it is one of the oldest sites in the monument. The site is situated in a high, deep cave nearly 1,000 feet in length. It was excavated by Earl H. Morris in 1923. Many artifacts of rare perishable materials were taken from this cave, providing valuable data on the early dwellers. Perhaps the most intriguing find was the Burial of the Hands. It consisted of the careful interment of a pair of hands and forearms with no other human remains present. Accompanying the burial were necklaces of abalone shell beads wrapped around the wrists and two pair of unworn sandals. Several fine baskets were also found with this unusual burial, one of which contained many small white beads. No one has been able to give a reasonable explanation for this unique burial.

Full-day canyon tours sometimes continue on up the canyon to two sites twenty-one miles from the visitors' center. These are known as **Mummy Cave** (Tse-ya-kin) (CDM-174) and **Massacre Cave** (CDM-176). Mummy Cave is one of the most awe-inspiring ruins in the monument. It is situated in two alcoves and on a joining ledge that lie over 300 feet above the canyon bottom. Most of the remaining structures are located on the ledge, which originally had fifteen rooms. Presently seven large rooms and a spectacular three-story tower remain on the ledge. The tower was restored by Earl Morris in 1924. The eastern alcove of Mummy Cave had approximately fifty-five rooms and four kivas, and the smaller western alcove had twenty rooms. Most of the rooms are from the Pueblo III period, with tree-ring dates from A.D. 1279 to 1284. A

Mummy Cave, main section is between two large alcoves in wall of Canyon del Muerto

very early date of A.D. 306 was also obtained from a beam in the eastern alcove, indicating that Mummy Cave was probably occupied for one thousand years. This site is visible from an overlook on the North Rim Drive.

Across the canyon from Mummy Cave is Massacre Cave (CDM-176). In 1805, more than one hundred Navajos who took refuge in this cave were killed by Spanish troops. This cave is situated 700 feet above the canyon floor and is best viewed from the Mummy Cave Overlook. No structures remain in this cave, but a low wall of stones can be seen where the Navajos sought refuge from the Spanish guns. A few petroglyphs and pictographs are also found at the site.

Canyon de Chelly National Monument covers 131 square miles and encompasses the floors and rims of the three major canyons: de Chelly, del Muerto, and Monument. Its ruins and beautiful vistas are strongly recommended to ruin buffs or anyone who appreciates the rugged grandeur of the Southwest.

In addition to the previously mentioned Cottonwood Campground, a good campground is located at Wheatfields Lake above the head of Canyon de Chelly on Arizona Highway No. 12 south of Lukachukai. It has drinking water, pit toilets, and barbeques. There is trout fishing in the lake, but a Navajo tribal permit is required.

126

No comprehensive report has been published of the prehistoric ruins of the Canyon de Chelly National Monument. The best written material is the book by Campbell Grant, *Canyon de Chelly: Its People and Rock Art,* published in 1978.

North of Canyon de Chelly is **Painted Cave,** which contains **Rotten Rock Ruin** in Hashbidibito Valley. Hashbidibito Creek is a tributary of Lukachukai Creek. The cave is six-tenths mile from the mouth of Buttress (Goldtooth's) Canyon. This cave and ruin are also on the Navajo Reservation.

The cave is named for a profusion of colored figures of humans, animals, and hands covering the back of the cave. The overall length of the cave is 270 feet, and it is 50 feet in width at its widest point. It is easily reached over a talus slope 100 feet above the valley floor. The ruin has a minimum of sixteen masonry rooms that were three stories high in some places. The walls are made of unshaped sandstone blocks laid up in heavy mortar. One kiva was found.

The cave was occupied in Basketmaker times starting about 400 A.D., and the later masonry structure was built by Pueblo III occupants. The one date from the later occupation was A.D. 1247. The cave was also used by Navajos in more recent years. Three Pueblo III burials containing many grave goods, including a cotton blanket, were discovered during excavations in the early 1940s by W. S. Fulton for the Amerind Foundation.

Ten miles south of Canyon de Chelly on a graded road is **Three Turkey Ruin Tribal Park*** (NA 174). It is in a narrow, 300-foot deep canyon known as Tse Deezhaai wash and Three Turkey Canyon. To reach this ruin, drive southeast from Thunderbird Lodge on Arizona Highway No. 7, which becomes gravel beyond the entrance to Spider Rock Overlook. Proceed about five miles on a good gravel road to a small directional sign, and turn right on a fair road for about five more miles to the ruin. The final few miles are quite rough and should not be traveled in bad weather or with trailers or large motor homes with long wheelbases.

This eighteen-room masonry ruin, situated in an overhang sixty feet above the canyon floor, is named for pictographs that resemble turkeys on the ruin wall. One large kiva is very well preserved at Three Turkey House. In 1938, Harold S. Colton of the Museum of Northern Arizona was the first scientist to visit this ruin, but certainly the Navajos in the area knew of it for several centuries. The site was occupied circa A.D. 1250 to 1310. Pottery found here indicates that the inhabitants were Anasazi from the

Three Turkey House, a small well preserved Anasazi ruin south of Canyon de Chelly on the Navajo Indian Reservation

Mesa Verde area who came into this region in the middle thirteenth century. Visitors cannot enter the ruin, but there is a beautiful view from a lookout across the canyon. Photographers should be sure to take a telephoto lens for the best pictures. A Navajo tribal campground that can best be described as "primitive" is located at the overlook. The camping fee is $1.50 per night. For persons interested in prehistoric ruins of the Southwest, the sight of this nearly virgin ruin in its wild setting is definitely worth the effort needed to reach it.

Kinlichee Ruin* "Red House" (NA 8022) is in the **Cross Canyon Group** (NA 8013) of ruins eight miles east of Ganado, Arizona, and two and one-half miles north of Cross Canyon Trading Post on a good gravel road. There is a direction sign at the turn-off on Arizona Highway No. 264 near Cross Canyon Trading Post. Kinlichee is situated across the canyon from the visitors' area on the canyon rim and on a spur of the talus slope. It is a masonry pueblo of seventy-five rooms and two kivas. Part of this ruin was two stories in height. Kinlichee proper has been only partially excavated and not restored. The six ruins at the visitors' area are small to medium in size and have been partially restored. A self-guided tour shows development of the Anasazi architecture at this site. The Pueblo occupation here was A.D. 1002 to 1024. A small campground is located on the hillside overlooking the ruins, but there is no drinking water. The ruins in the visitors' area are partially covered, but in spite of this, water erosion has damaged the walls of the masonry rooms and the large kiva.

One mile west of Ganado, Arizona, is **Hubbell Trading Post National Historic Site.*** This restored Indian trading post was started 100 years ago by Don Lorenzo Hubbell, one of the best-known and most successful Indian traders of the late nineteenth century. He built a trading empire that included stage and freight lines in addition to several trading posts and other enterprises. Hubbell was a good friend to the Navajos and contributed much to the encouragement and improvement of the quality of weaving and silverwork in this area. Hubbell died in 1930 and is buried on the small hill overlooking his trading post. Navajo women can often be seen weaving rugs in the large, barnlike building at Hubbell's as they did when he was alive. This historic site is open daily from 8:00 AM to 5:00 PM except Thanksgiving, Christmas, and New Year's Day. The address of Hubbell's is Box 150, Ganado, Arizona 86505. This, of course, is not a prehistoric site, but it is included in this guide because it is interesting and should be seen while visiting this area of the Navajo Reservation.

Hubbell Trading Post National Historic Site, Ganado, Arizona

Map 12

Prehistoric Ruins of the Kayenta Area

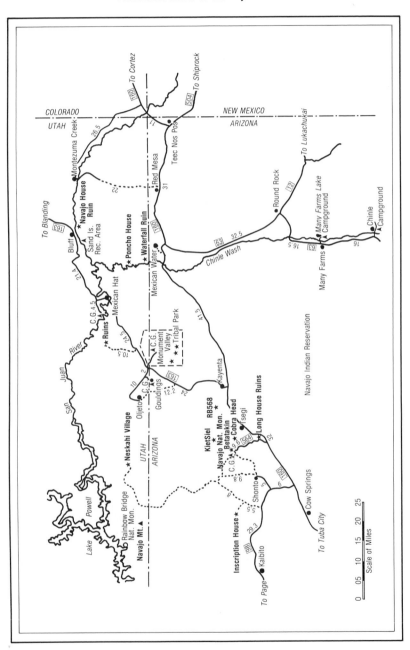

XI

Kayenta Area

The small Navajo town of Kayenta is located in northeastern Arizona near the Utah border. It is on Navajo Route No. 1 (U.S. Highway 160), the main road connecting Flagstaff with the towns in southeastern Utah and southwestern Colorado. This area is locally known as the Four Corners because the corners of the four states of Utah, Colorado, New Mexico, and Arizona form the only point common to four states in the United States. This area extends up into the corner of Utah south of the San Juan River. The entire area is on the Navajo Indian Reservation. There are two motels at Kayenta; the Wetherill Inn and the Holiday Inn, and other services are available. Several campgrounds are also in the vicinity. The locations of the ruins in the Kayenta area are shown on Map #12. All of the ruins in this area are Anasazi.

The outstanding restored ruins in the Kayenta area are those in Navajo National Monument,* twenty-two miles southwest of Kayenta. These are some of the most beautiful and interesting prehistoric ruins in the Southwest due to their physical setting and their excellent state of preservation. They are not as well-known as some ruins, such as those in Mesa Verde, but they are truly memorable to anyone fortunate enough to visit them.

To reach Navajo National Monument from Tuba City, Arizona, drive fifty miles northeast on Navajo Route No. 1 (U.S. 160) to a directional sign, then nine miles west on a paved entrance road to the monument headquarters. The three major ruins at Navajo National Monument are Betatakin, Kiet Siel, and Inscription House.

Betatakin* (NA 2515) is in a canyon near the monument headquarters. It can be seen from an overlook at the end of short Sandal Trail, which starts at the visitors' center. A steep trail descends over 700 feet into the canyon and affords a spectacular close-up view of this ruin. Guided ranger walking tours of about three hours to Betatakin leave the visitors' center at 8:30 AM and 1:30 PM. These tours are limited to twenty persons, so it is wise to be early during the summer months. (Be sure to check the local time, because in recent years the state of Arizona has been on standard time, but the national parks and monuments have been on daylight saving time.)

Betatakin is a masonry structure of over 135 rooms built in an immense alcove 500 feet in height. It was partially excavated and stabilized by Neil M. Judd in 1917 and has been well maintained by the park service since then. Visitors on the ranger tours may enter the ruin, and opportunities for taking pictures are excellent. It is interesting to note that this extensive ruin was occupied from only A.D. 1248 to 1286. As with most other southwestern ruins, it is not definitely known why Betatakin was abandoned.

Betatakin Ruin, situated in a huge alcove in Tsegi Canyon, Navajo National Monument

High rooms at end of Betatakin Ruin, Navajo National Monument

Milling bins used by the Anasazi to grind corn, Betatakin Ruin

Petroglyphs of an animal and a human on canyon wall at Betatakin, Navajo National Monument

Kiet Siel* (NA 2519) means "broken pottery" in the Navajo language. This ruin is eight miles by trail from the visitors' center and may only be reached by foot or on horseback. Backpackers must register at the visitors' center and may camp overnight at Kiet Siel when a ranger is in attendance at the ruin. Those wishing to rent horses and take the ranger-guided trip to Kiet Siel may do so at the visitors' center, at least one day in advance. The horseback trip takes one day and is fun for able-bodied persons of all ages, in spite of the sore muscles of those not accustomed to riding a horse. My family rates this one of their favorites among many enjoyable excursions to southwestern ruins.

Kiet Siel is a masonry and jacal ruin of 160 rooms, many in an excellent state of preservation, some with their original roofs. The ruin is situated in a very long cave or alcove roofed by a "billowing" cliff streaked with desert varnish and blackened by the soot of ancient fires. Limited numbers of persons may enter the ruin via a park service ladder. Walking through the long-deserted streets and courtyards is an unforgettable experience. This ruin was excavated and stabilized by the National Park Service in 1934. Kiet Siel was occupied from circa A.D. 1109 to 1285.

Inscription House* (NA 2160) is in Nitsin Canyon thirty-five miles by road from the visitors' center. It is reached by a five-mile round-trip trail that begins at the end of the road. The ruin is named for an inscription found in 1909. It was believed for many years that the inscription included the date 1661, indicating a Spanish visit to this site. Now it is generally accepted that the date is 1861. This ruin has been closed to the public for several years because it is quite fragile and has needed stabilization. It is planned to re-open it in 1981.

Inscription House is an eighty-room, three-storied structure of adobe, masonry, and jacal construction. Only one kiva is present. Because of the extensive use of adobe in its construction, the elements and erosion of visitors have damaged it more than the better-protected and more resistant masonry at Betatakin and Kiet Siel. Inscription House has some "T"-shaped doors, and it was inhabited

South end of Long House Ruin in Long House Valley, Navajo Indian Reservation

from A.D. 1250 to 1300. This ruin was excavated by Byron Cummings in 1914 to 1916 and in 1930 and 1966 by George Gumerman, who uncovered thirty-two human burials and ten rooms.

The visitors' center at Navajo National Monument is open year-round from 8:00 AM to 5:00 PM. It includes exhibits, a slide show, and a gift shop. The visitors' center and exhibits are accessible to persons in wheelchairs, but unfortunately the ruins are not.

There is a very nice small but modern campground near the visitors' center. Rangers give campfire talks during the summer months. If the regular campground is full, inquire about the old "dry" campground nearby. No food or automotive supplies are available here, so travelers should stock up before leaving Kayenta or Tuba City. The monument address is Tonalea, Arizona 86044.

North of the entrance road to Navajo National Monument, in Longhouse Valley, is **Long House Ruin** (NA 897). It is four miles southeast of the mouth of Tsegi Canyon on a low ridge. Another ruin, known as **Pottery Hill,** is located on the north side of Long House Valley about three miles south of Marsh Pass. Long House Ruin is a long, narrow surface pueblo of ninety by ten feet. Some remaining walls stand ten feet high. Other smaller structures nearby are apparently part of this site. This ruin has not been excavated, but potsherds of a great variety have been found on the surface. The one date for this site is A.D. 1274.

Cobra Head Ruin (RB 1006) is situated on an elongated fossil sand dune on the east side of Cobra wash. The Cobra Head is four miles west of Marsh Pass in Tsegi Canyon. The site is composed of four pithouse-type structures, two small surface masonry units, and several storage cists. Cobra Head Ruin dates from the Developmental Pueblo period and was excavated by the Rainbow Bridge Expedition under the direction of Ralph L. Beals in 1937 to 1938. Camping is available nearby at Navajo National Monument.

Another ruin in this area is known as **RB 568.** It is seven miles northwest of Kayenta in Kaycuddie wash, an intermittent stream flowing east and south from Skeleton Mesa and entering Laguna Creek at a point about halfway between Marsh Pass and Kayenta. The rooms of this ruin are organized in three groups. Group I rooms were built against the bluff. The main group was a cluster of rooms centered on a rock ledge flanked by bluffs on the east and west and by a steeply raising rock behind. This ruin has an estimated 100 rooms constructed of haphazard slab masonry. A number of burials were found 250 feet to the south. George W. Brainerd excavated this site in 1936, and it has been dated at A.D. 1200 to 1275.

Monument Valley Tribal Park* is on the Navajo Reservation northeast of Kayenta along the Arizona–Utah border. A recent survey by the Museum of Northern Arizona lists many sites in the valley and its associated canyons. These sites include open sites on sand dunes, canyon bottoms, mesa tops, and other locations; sheltered sites in alcoves, at cliff bases, and in overhangs; and cliff sites in caves, on ledges, or on overhangs above ground level. There are also a number of small petroglyph sites in these valleys.

One ruin in the Tse Biyi Canyon is known as **Echo Cave** (NA 8097). It has unusual round structures, and the cave reportedly has eight to sixteen separate echoes. Another ruin in Tse Biyi Canyon was named **Flute Player House** (NA 8107) by Guernsey in 1919. Four other named ruins to the west in Mystery Valley are **Pictograph Cave** (NA 8067), **Firestick House** (NA 8065), **Cliff House** (NA 8241), and **Burial Cave** (NA 8237).

The ruins in Monument Valley can be visited by taking guided tours from the visitors' center at the tribal park or from Goulding's Trading Post and Lodge. There is a KOA Campground at Goulding's. Goulding's is open from March 15 to November 1; the telephone number is (801) 727-3231. The address is Box 1, Monument Valley, Utah 84536. The road into the visitors' center leaves U.S. Highway No. 163 near the Arizona–Utah border. The sign that warns "travel at your own risk" should be heeded. This road can be deceptively bad, and it is best not to take pickup campers, motor homes, or trailers over it. Monument Valley does have spectacular rock formations and is a favorite place for picture taking.

Neskahi Village (NA 7719) is located on Paiute Mesa five miles north of the Utah–Arizona line in Utah. It is near the west bank of Neskahi wash at the end of a forested ridge. This site consists of a small "D"-shaped masonry pueblo of seven rooms, eighteen pithouses, and two kivas. It dates from A.D. 1070 to the late 1200s and was excavated by Glen Canyon Project personnel in 1961. Another site, named **Pottery Pueblo,** is three miles northeast of Neskahi Village.

Poncho House (NA 8233) is in southeastern Utah on the east bank of Chinle wash. It is nine to ten miles above (south of) the confluence of Chinle wash with the San Juan River. The ruin is situated at a point where the wash bends sharply, forming a cove, and a good spring is located at the site. Poncho House can be reached by vehicle from Mexican Hat, Utah, but it is best to hire a local guide or take a guided tour from Goulding's Lodge, north of Kayenta.

Poncho House is probably the largest and most impressive unexcavated cliff ruin in the Southwest. It was constructed on several levels. One part was built on the base of the cliff and extends up onto the talus slope. The main remaining portions are in the high natural alcoves protected by the overhangs. The total number of rooms in all sections was at least two hundred. Water erosion has destroyed some of the earlier lower sections. and the western section has been badly damaged by pothunters. Other than the work by Samuel Guernsey in 1922, no scientific excavation has been conducted here. This ruin is one of the best examples of an endangered site. If something is not done to protect it, vandals and nature will reduce it to rubble and eliminate its scientific and aesthetic value in a few years.

Also in Chinle wash is **Waterfall Ruin**, northwest of Mexican Water, Arizona, near the trading post of Nakaito and close to the Arizona–Utah line. It is situated in a shallow cave above the valley floor where the Chinle wash makes an abrupt turn. Waterfall is a medium-sized, multicomponent site. Early pithouses underlie a masonry structure. The ruin is not well preserved. It has been damaged by weathering, seepage from two springs, and some pothunting. The site dates from Basketmaker III to Pueblo II times, according to Guernsey, who did some excavation here in 1922. About fifteen miles upstream from Waterfall Ruin is a small ruin known as **Ford House**. There are pictographs on nearby canyon walls.

Betatakin Ruin Navajo National Monument

Ruins in Yucca Cave, Canyon del Muerto

Map 13

Prehistoric Ruins of the Canyonlands

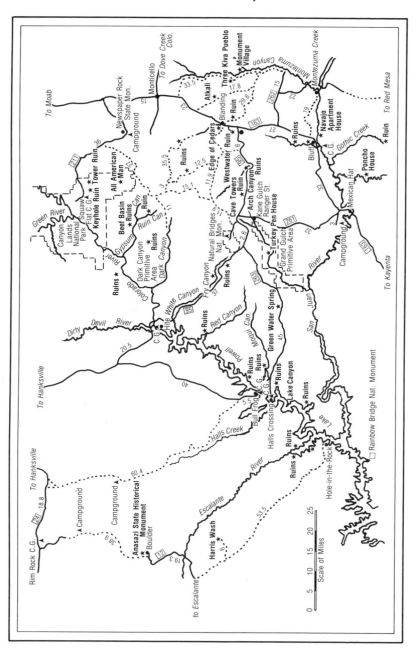

XII

Canyonlands Area

In the southeastern part of Utah lies Lake Powell, formed by Glen Canyon Dam on the Colorado River near Page, Arizona. This huge lake provides many recreational opportunities, including boating, fishing, water skiing, and exploring the rock canyons and ruins along the shoreline. The side canyons with some of the most extensive ruins are Escalante, Lake Canyon, and Moki Canyon. The ruins in the side canyons are most easily accessible by boats that can be rented at Wahweap near Glen Canyon Dam, Hall's Crossing, and Hite, Utah, near the north end of the lake. There are campgrounds and supplies at all of these marinas.

A number of small prehistoric ruins lie within **Canyonlands National Park**, which is located along the Colorado River north of Glen Canyon Dam. However, the major sites open to the public are south of the park in the canyons emptying into the San Juan River from the north. These sites are in San Juan County, Utah. Some good campgrounds are located in this area, and the towns of Monticello, Blanding, and Bluff have lodging and other services.

This area is a good place for people who want to get away from crowds and visit ruins that are not swarmed over by thousands of tourists. Campers and four-wheel drive enthusiasts will find many miles of trails and challenging roads in this beautiful red-rock country. A former ranger in this area, Edward Abbey, has written a book titled *Desert Solitaire*. This work is recommended to those who appreciate this country and its stark beauty.

The ruins in this area are generally not well marked, and in some cases, little excavation or restoration has been done on them. Many of the ruins are accessible only by foot, horseback, or four-wheel drive vehicle, so if you want to stay in your car, you had better go elsewhere. The hiking or climbing required to reach a site may make it more memorable and desirable to the avid ruin buff. Therefore, this area is highly recommended to the able-bodied hiker and adventurer who wants to search out ruins seen by few others. Locations of the prehistoric ruins in the Canyonlands are shown on Map #13.

Several ruins are located in the vicinity of Blanding, Utah. One of these is on the northwest edge of this town. There are directional signs in town, or you can ask for directions to **Edge of the Cedars Pueblo.*** This is an Anasazi pueblo of masonry construction and was inhabited from A.D. 750 to 1150. This pueblo had fifty to one hundred rooms and several kivas. One of the kivas has been excavated and restored. The prehistoric population obtained water from nearby Westwater Canyon, where another pueblo ruin is located. It is thought that Edge of the Cedars may have been a prehistoric trade center. This site is being excavated and restored by personnel from Brigham Young University. A cultural center has been built near the pueblo, and it will include exhibits of some of the artifacts found during the excavations.

Southwest of Blanding is another prehistoric site called **Westwater Ruin*** (also known as **Five Kiva House**). To reach this site, travel 1.6 miles south of Blanding on U.S. Highway No. 163, then turn west on a paved road, and travel 1.7 miles to Westwater Ruin and Natural Bridge. This cliff dwelling had twenty rooms, five kivas, small storage units, and several open work areas. This Pueblo III ruin has been badly damaged by vandals, making it useless for scientific study and less interesting to visitors. On the road to the ruin, a small natural bridge may be seen at the right.

Cave Towers Ruin* is located twenty-five miles southwest of Blanding via U.S. Highway No. 163 and Utah Highway No. 95. It is situated at the head of Mule Canyon. The site consists of seven round towers arranged in a semicircle on a high canyon rim. Three of these towers are visible from below. Directly below the towers is a cave in the canyon wall. The site also includes a cliff site, storage rooms, living structures, and a kiva. Cave Towers has not been excavated, but it is estimated that it was occupied from A.D. 1050 to 1150.

Arch Canyon Ruin* may be visited by hiking up Comb Wash

142

Restored kiva with ladder entrance in the roof, Edge of the Cedars Ruin, Blanding, Utah

Excavated Anasazi pueblo at Edge of the Cedars Ruin, Blanding, Utah

143

a short distance to Arch Canyon. Comb wash crosses Utah Highway No. 95 about twenty-two miles southwest of Blanding, Utah. Turn north on a dirt road that parallels Comb wash, and travel about four miles north. This small Anasazi pueblo site is administered by the Bureau of Land Management.

To reach **Grand Gulch Primitive Area,**[*] drive thirty-four miles southwest of Blanding via U.S. Highway No. 163 and Utah Highway No. 95, then two miles south on Utah Highway No. 261 to Kane Gulch. Because this is a primitive area, visitors must travel by foot or horseback. You are required to register at the Kane Gulch Ranger Station or a sheriff's office. It is about a five-hour hike from Kane Gulch into Grand Gulch. There are many Anasazi ruins in Grand Gulch, some of which are well preserved. One of the few named ruins is called TURKEY PEN HOUSE. The ruins range in time from Basketmaker III to Pueblo III. Richard Wetherill, a pioneer rancher and explorer, excavated ruins in Grand Gulch in the 1880s. He found some of the first evidence of Basketmaker culture below the more recent Pueblo materials. Grand Gulch is a fine area for the active traveler who wants a strenuous hike through a primitive canyon with some interesting and little-known ruins. When hiking in this area, be sure to carry plenty of water. It is a hot and dry country much of the year.

Northeast of Blanding is the well-known site named **Alkali Ridge.** Sites are located at varying distances on either side of the road for about eight miles. The mesa top has numerous sites, from Basketmaker pithouses to Pueblo III surface masonry structures. All of these have been backfilled and are indicated by low mounds and sherd areas. In 1931 to 1933, J. O. Brew excavated a total of 234 rooms and 10 trash mounds in 13 sites. At Site No. 13, a pithouse was dated at A.D. 741 to 777. Brew's final report on Alkali Ridge is a very interesting and well-written thesis concerning this area of the Southwest (Brew, 1946).

Northeast of Blanding are three recently excavated prehistoric sites known as Monument Village, Montezuma Village, and Three Kiva Pueblo.

Monument Village (42S A971) is located on a rise of ground at the convergence of Monument and Montezuma canyons. This site is composed primarily of Pueblo I pithouses. It also contains three groups of contiguous masonry surface rooms totaling thirty-eight. The occupation of this site also extends back to Basketmaker III times. It was excavated by Ray Matheny of Brigham Young University in 1961, 1963, 1965, and 1969 to 1971.

Three Kiva Pueblo* (42S A863) is approximately twenty-two miles down Montezuma Canyon from Monticello, Utah, on a dirt road. The main structure is a masonry pueblo of fourteen rooms and three kivas built during several construction phases. It is eighteen by twelve yards in size. Peripheral features include a trash mound to the southeast, a ramada area to the west, and a long, narrow room, or "turkey run" on the south side. There are other small sites in the area and a polychrome pictograph about one mile south on the west side of the streambed. This site dates from late Pueblo I through Pueblo III. It was excavated in 1969, 1971, and 1972 by Ray Matheny. There are several campgrounds a few miles west of Monticello, Utah.

Montezuma Village* is in Montezuma Canyon several miles upcanyon from Three Kiva Pueblo. It is a multistoried masonry structure containing over 150 rooms and kivas and encompassing numerous outlying components. This site has not been well studied.

Canyonlands National Park* is located in northwestern San Juan County, Utah. To reach the Needles area, where most of the ruins are located, drive west on Utah Highway No. 211, which leaves U.S. Highway No. 163 about twelve miles north of Monticello. Proceed northwest for thirty-six miles to the Squaw Flat Ranger Station. Two major sites in this area are Tower Ruin* and Keyhole Ruin,* five miles southeast of the ranger station on a dirt road, near Squaw Buttes.

In the Needles area are many small ruins and petroglyphs. A polychrome petroglyph, named All-American Man,* is found in Salt Creek Canyon. Directions and maps to guide the traveler to this petroglyph and the ruins named above can be obtained at the Squaw Flat Ranger Station.

Other ruins are located to the north in the Moab section of the park. These ruins include dwelling rooms, kivas, and granaries. The unpaved roads in this section are mostly graded dirt and are slippery when wet. This is an excellent area for four-wheel drive vehicles. The park is free and is open year-round at all times. The ruins in Canyonlands date from A.D. 900 to 1200, but little scientific study has been done. A National Park Service campground is located near the Squaw Flat Ranger Station.

Other lesser-known and unstudied ruins in this area are located in Ruin Canyon west of Monticello, in Fry Canyon on Utah Highway No. 95 northwest of Natural Bridges National Monument, and at Green Water Spring on Utah Highway No. 263, southwest of the monument. A number of small ruins are located in **Natural Bridges National Monument.*** These can be found by obtaining directions from the personnel on duty.

West of the Colorado River in Garfield County is **Anasazi State Historical Monument.*** The monument is two miles north of Boulder, Utah. This site consists of jacal living units and masonry storage structures. Part of this site is named the **Coombs Site,** which was inhabited from A.D. 1075 to 1275. It was excavated by Robert Lister for the University of Utah, and part of it was stabilized. Calf Creek Recreation Area, which includes a campground, is thirteen miles south of Boulder, Utah.

Thirty miles northwest of Monticello, Utah, is **Ruin Park***; it is between Elk Ridge and the Colorado River to the west. A number of sites from Pueblo II and Pueblo III times are located in this area. The inhabitants of many of these sites were Mesa Verde Anasazi.

The largest site in Ruin Park is on the north side of the west end of the park. This site, known as **LS 13-2,** is a "U"-shaped masonry structure that was three stories high in some places. The walls are built of unworked sandstone blocks laid up in sparse mortar. The structure measures fifteen by eleven meters and has an opening in the east side. There is no kiva in evidence. About twenty-five meters east of the main building is the base of a small, double-walled tower.

One of the northernmost ruins of the Mesa Verde culture is **Fort Bottom Ruin.** The site is located on a small butte in a sharp turn in the Colorado River. It is connected to the wall of the canyon by a very narrow ridge. There are two rooms in the main "fort" structure and one second-story room. The walls were made of unshaped sandstone blocks laid up without mortar and were plastered on the interior. Several small structures surround the main structure.

Directions to the ruins in Ruin Park and nearby areas may be obtained from the ranger at the Squaw Flat Ranger Station. This is wild, rough country, and persons not familiar with the area should not venture out alone.

One of the most spectacular rock art sites in the Southwest is known as the **Great Gallery*** in Barrier Canyon, also known as Horseshoe Canyon. The site is located in Canyonlands National Recreation Area, west of the Colorado River. This outstanding panel of petroglyphs is on the north side of Barrier Canyon four miles above the spot where the four-wheel drive road crosses it. The petroglyphs are in a rock shelter and run for a distance of thirty meters along its back wall. The main designs are large, red, anthropomorphic figures, some of which are life-size. In addition to these large figures are smaller human and animal figures. The large figures are of two types: solid red persons with narrow, round shoulders, and broad-shouldered figures with very elaborate and detailed decoration in red, white, and green. The only facial features are large, round eyes. The smaller elements include humans, animals such as antelope and dogs, and a humpbacked flute player. These panels have been carefully reproduced in a mural in the Utah State Museum.

Other ruins in this area are located in western side canyons of the Colorado River. In Nine Mile Canyon, one of the more extensive and well-preserved ruins is **Nordell's Fort,** probably the largest site in this canyon. It is situated on the ridge that forms the junction of Nine Mile and Devil's canyons. Two ruins in Hill Creek Canyon are **Fortification Rock (Long Mesa)** and **Rock House (Eight Mile Ruin)**; the latter is the most extensive group of open structures in the area. Rock House is on the west rim of Hill Creek Canyon south of a side canyon about eleven miles below the mouth of Horsecorn Canyon. Directions and current road conditions concerning the ruins in Nine Mile Canyon can be obtained in Price, Utah. The ruins in Hill Creek Canyon are difficult to reach, and a guide should be hired. Descriptions and locations of the major petroglyph and pictograph sites in southwestern Utah may be found in *Petroglyphs and Pictographs of Utah: Volume II* by Kenneth Castleton.

Map 14

Prehistoric Ruins of the Mesa Verde Area

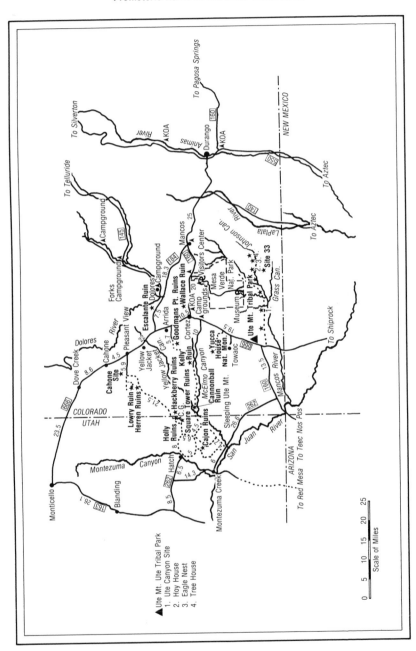

▲ Ute Mt. Ute Tribal Park
1. Ute Canyon Site
2. Hoy House
3. Eagle Nest
4. Tree House

Scale of Miles
0 5 10 15 20 25

XIII

Mesa Verde Area

This area is in southwestern Colorado and extreme south-eastern Utah. The ruins in this area can be visited from Cortez, Colorado, or by camping. Some of the better preserved sites are in Hovenweep National Monument in Colorado and Utah. The ruins in this section are generally reached by gravel roads that are easily traveled except in very bad weather. Two ruins outside of Hovenweep National Monument that have been excavated and restored are Lowry Ruin, west of Pleasant View, and Escalante Ruin, near Dolores, Colorado.

As in other areas, persons wishing to visit ruins on private land should obtain permission of the owner or tenant. This area is rather sparsely populated, and directions to unmarked ruins should be sought locally. Map #14 contains the locations of ruins and other features in the Mesa Verde area.

Hovenweep National Monument* is in Montezuma County, Colorado, and San Juan County, Utah. The headquarters is forty miles west of Cortez, Colorado, and twenty-seven miles southwest of Pleasant View, Colorado. The best route from the east is the graded road west from Pleasant View, about seven miles, then follow the directional signs to monument headquarters. From the west, take Utah Highway No. 262 east between Blanding and Bluff, Utah, to a graded gravel road to Square Tower Group.

Small visitors center at Hovenweep National Monument, Utah

The monument consists of six separate groups of ruins: **Square Tower** and **Cajon** in Utah and **Holly Canyon**, **Hackberry Canyon**, **Cutthroat Castle**, and **Goodman Point** in Colorado. Square Tower, Holly, and Hackberry are the most accessible from the visitors' center and therefore are the most frequently visited. Cutthroat Castle and Goodman Point are more remote from the headquarters. Goodman Point is at the head of Goodman Canyon. To reach it take the county road 2 miles south of Arriola, Colorado and travel five miles west. The site is on the left near the canyon rim. It is advisable to start at the monument headquarters and obtain directions to the other groups. Inquiries concerning Hovenweep should be addressed to: Superintendent, Mesa Verde National Park, Colorado 81330.

The ruins in Hovenweep are typified by oval, circular, and "D"-shaped towers at the heads of small canyons. Living units of various sizes are also associated with the towers. These structures are built of excellent stone-coursed masonry. The functions of the towers are not known, but they may have been lookouts or defensive structures to guard the precious springs in the canyons.

Square Tower Group has an interesting self-guided trail that leads around the canyon rim and into the canyon to the tower for which the group is named. The largest structure of this group,

150

Hovenweep Castle, has two towers, two kivas, and numerous dwelling rooms. Walls up to twenty feet high are still standing at this imposing building. There is a tiny visitors' center with a few exhibits at Square Tower. The ranger here, as at most remote monuments, is very willing and able to answer questions of travelers.

This monument and its major features are not accessible to handicapped persons. Hovenweep has a campground but no firewood. Neither are food, gasoline, or other supplies available at Hovenweep. It is an uncrowded and quiet place to camp and enjoy the evidence of prehistoric man. For the energetic, a trail leads from Square Tower to Holly and Hackberry canyons.

Little scientific excavation has been conducted at Hovenweep, but the pottery indicates that the site was occupied circa A.D. 1200 to 1400. Unfortunately, there is no good written source of information about Hovenweep. Joseph Winter's work has begun to provide some answers (Winter, 1975).

Hovenweep National Monument is strongly recommended to those who want to see a well-preserved group of ruins that are still in a setting similar to that of the prehistoric inhabitants. This is an out-of-the-way place, but it is worth the effort to reach it.

Hovenweep Castle, largest structure at Square Tower Group, Hovenweep National Monument

Square Tower for which Square Tower Group is
named, other towers are round or D-shaped

Another site in this area is owned by George Kelly. It is referred to here as **Kelly Ruin.*** George Kelly is a retired horticul-
turist who has lived in McElmo Canyon since 1965. Kelly Ruin is
located in McElmo Canyon west of Cortez, Colorado. To reach
this ruin, travel three miles south of Cortez on U.S. Highway 666 to
the McElmo Canyon road, also known as County Road "G." Turn
west on this road, and go ten miles to the Kelly's mailbox on the
right side of the road. Turn right on the dirt road, and go one mile
to the end. The Kellys have a small orchard near their pueblo-style
home.

Kelly Ruin is a Pueblo III masonry ruin of undetermined size. Mr. Kelly has been excavating this ruin on a part-time basis for thirteen years. He has uncovered about twenty-five rooms, two kivas, and a masonry column of unknown function. A small masonry room is also located in an alcove in the canyon wall behind the ruin. The two kivas have been restored, and visitors may enter them by descending a short ladder through an opening in the roof. The column, which was found below the present ground level, is about six feet in height and three feet in diameter at the base. Mr. Kelly believes that further excavation may uncover other columns and reveal their purpose. Some of the artifacts found in the kivas have been left in place, and others are preserved in the Kellys' home. Mr. Kelly and his wife, Sue, are home most of the time, but it is advisable to call from Cortez before driving out to the site. Visiting this site not only provides the opportunity to see an interesting ruin, but also to meet two hospitable people.

Cannonball Ruin is at the head of a small canyon that is a tributary of Yellowjacket Canyon, the most northern considerable tributary of McElmo Creek west of Cortez, Colorado. The ruin consists of two pueblos on opposite sides of the canyon and a

Masonry rooms at Lowry Ruin, Colorado, Sleeping Ute Mountain in the background

square tower built upon a detached rock in the bed of the canyon. The southern pueblo is 114 feet by 72 feet in size and has six kivas and a tower. It was excavated in 1908 by Sylvanus Morley and dates from Pueblo III times. The northern pueblo has not been excavated.

Another interesting site in this area is **Lowry Ruin**,* located nine miles west of Pleasant View, Colorado, on a graded gravel road. This excavated and well-restored ruin is a masonry pueblo of forty rooms, eight small kivas, and a detached great kiva. One of the small kivas has painted decorations and has been restored and protected. Lowry Ruin was occupied intermittently from A.D.

Unique painted kiva with masonry pilasters supporting pole "shelves", Lowry Ruin, Colorado

1090 to 1240 and was modified considerably during this period. An easy self-guided trail takes the visitor to various parts of the city. The ruin was named for George Lowry, an early homesteader, and became a national historical monument in 1967. Lowry was first excavated by Paul Martin in the early 1930s. It was reexcavated in 1965, and in 1975 the ruin was stabilized and the painted kiva restored. The great kiva has been partially restored and provides a good example of one of these large ceremonial structures.

Excavated and stabilized pueblo rooms at Lowry Ruin near Pleasant View, Colorado

Lowry does not have a campground, but there are picnic tables. My family and I spent a night here in a self-contained camper, and the sight of this pueblo ruin in the light of a full moon will remain with us always. Lowry is a good place to visit for a few hours because it is easily accessible and is seldom crowded. Many unnamed ruins are located on the nearby mesas.

Herren Ruins is a large masonry pueblo of thirteen house units. Each unit has habitation rooms, kivas, round towers, and refuse heaps. It is a Pueblo III site and is west of Pleasant View on the north side of Ruin Canyon. The site is one mile west of the old Ruin Canyon post office. In 1928, Paul Martin of the Field Museum excavated twenty-six rooms, four towers, and two kivas here.

Five airline miles from Herren Ruins is the site known as **Little Dog Ruins**. Little Dog is a Pueblo II site composed of several masonry pueblos, pithouse structures, kivas, and towers. It was excavated by Paul S. Martin in 1929.

Bear Tooth Ruin is located west of Pleasant View on the north rim of Ruin Canyon. The mound of this ruin is 35 feet wide, 100 feet long, and 15 feet high. The site was a sandstone masonry pueblo of twenty-two rooms and two kivas. Some parts of it were two or three stories in height. This ruin was primarily a Pueblo III site and was excavated by Martin in 1929.

Cahone Canyon Site I is approximately twenty-six miles northwest of Cortez, Colorado, and seven miles west of Pleasant View. It is one mile north of Cahone Canyon. This was a masonry pueblo with two large kivas, seventy-five to one hundred rooms, and fifteen small kivas. The site, which dates from A.D. 386 to 872, was excavated by Paul Martin in 1937. **Cahone Canyon Site II** is nearby. Herren, Little Dog, Bear Tooth, and the Cahone sites are on private property, and permission should be obtained to visit them.

A recently excavated and restored site is **Escalante Ruin*** (5MT2149), located west of the town of Dolores, Colorado, on the most prominent hill south of the Dolores River. To reach it, drive

On a hill near Dolores, Colorado is Escalante Ruin first seen by Europeans in 1776

one and one-half miles south of Dolores on Colorado Highway No. 145, turn right on Colorado Highway No. 147, and go about one mile to the Escalante sign.

The main part of the site is a Chaco-style pueblo on the top of a steep hill. A large Chaco-type kiva, over twenty-five feet in diameter, has a subfloor ventilator and eight pilasters. Surrounding the kiva are dwelling and storage rooms. The rooms are considerably

Dominguez Ruin, a small Mesa Verde site near Escalante Ruin

larger than those of the Mesa Verde–type structures in the vicinity. There is a beautiful view of the Dolores Valley, Mesa Verde to the south, and Sleeping Ute Mountain to the southwest.

At the foot of the hill, near the parking lot, is a small Mesa Verde–style structure known as **Dominguez Ruin.*** It is contemporaneous with the hilltop Chaco pueblo, and apparently the people of these two branches of the Anasazi dwelled together at this site. Escalante Ruin was occupied for only ten or fifteen years during the period A.D. 1130 to 1145. The site was named for Fray Velez de Escalante, who traveled through this area in the summer of 1776 and probably observed this ruin. Escalante Ruin was excavated by Al Lancaster for the Bureau of Land Management in 1975. It was dedicated as a national historic site in 1976. The site has picnic facilities and restrooms but no camping spaces. Persons in wheelchairs can visit Dominguez Ruin, but the trail up to Escalante is not accessible.

Mesa Verde National Park,* in the center of this area, includes the best known and most visited prehistoric ruins of the Southwest. Mesa Verde certainly has some of the most interesting and best-preserved ruins in this part of the country. A visit to this park is a "must" for anyone who wants to understand and appreciate the Anasazi culture.

The popularity of and extensive facilities at Mesa Verde have contributed to conditions that make it difficult to fully appreciate the beauty of the prehistoric remains of this area. When thousands of people traipse through a ruin every day, it can lose its appeal, and the many footsteps literally erode the centuries-old pathways. To avoid the crowds, you should try to visit Mesa Verde in the spring or fall, when the numbers of visitors are much smaller. At these times the park personnel have more time to be courteous and answer individual questions and requests.

Visitors to Mesa Verde may camp at Morfield Campground, the one facility in the park, but it is often crowded. Other campgrounds on U.S. Highway No. 160 between Durango and Cortez, Colorado, often fill during the summer months. Therefore, it is advisable to make reservations or stop early in the day to be assured of a campsite. Lodging is available in the park at the modern Far View Motor Lodge. For reservations, write to the Mesa Verde Company, Mesa Verde National Park, Colorado 81330 (telephone: 303-529-4421). Cortez and Durango have a number of good motel accommodations, and these are good points from which to visit the ruins of this area. The Durango library has displays of prehistoric artifacts of this vicinity, and several good Indian arts and crafts stores are located in these towns.

Scenic Morfield Campground in Mesa Verde National Park

Durango is the southern terminus of a narrow-gauge railroad that runs, during the summer months, to the old mining town of Silverton in the San Juan Mountains. This day-long round trip traverses some of the best mountain scenery in the Southwest and is enjoyable for children and adults of all ages. Reservations are usually needed for a trip on this popular ride, but it is a great opportunity to take color photographs of the mountain scenery. The train will stop at some spots to let off or pick up fishermen and backpackers.

Mesa Verde National Park is located in southwestern Colorado. The park entrance is ten miles east of Cortez, Colorado, on U.S. Highway No. 160. The main ruins area is twenty miles south of the entrance. Bus tours are available from major towns in the area. The archeological museum, Navajo Hill Visitor Center, and the trail to Spruce Tree House are accessible to wheelchairs with some assistance.

There are an estimated 3,200 prehistoric sites in this huge park. The great number of outstanding excavated ruins make it impossible to describe them in this guide. The most spectacular ruins are situated in caves in the canyon walls. Those in the vicinity of Chapin Mesa, the main visitor area, include **Cliff Palace,*** **Spruce Tree House,*** **Square Tower House,*** and **Balcony House.*** The

Spruce Tree House is easily accessible from the visitors area on Chapin Mesa, Mesa Verde Nat. Park

Circular kivas and rooms, Far View House on top of Chapin
Mesa, Mesa Verde National Park

Pipe Shrine House viewed from Far View House, Chapin Mesa

first three may be seen by taking short trails. Visiting Balcony House requires climbing a ladder, which is fun for children but not for persons who are disabled or afraid of heights. Cliff Palace, the largest ruin in the park, had 220 rooms. Chapin Mesa contains the park headquarters, museum, and other tourist facilities near Spruce Tree House. The larger mesatop ruins with the number of rooms in parentheses are **Far View House*** (fifty), **Sun Point Pueblo*** (twenty), **Cedar Tree Tower*** (tower and kiva), and **Pipe Shrine House** (twenty-two). The earliest sites are Basketmaker pithouses, most of which are unexcavated.

The most recent section of Mesa Verde opened to the public is Wetherill Mesa, lying in the southwest corner of the park. Since the late 1950s, archeologists have been excavating some of the ruins in this section. In 1972, Wetherill was opened to the public on a controlled basis. Private vehicles are not allowed on Wetherill; all visitors must travel in guided groups. Visitors board free buses that leave the parking lot at Far View Visitors' Center every one-half hour. They then take a one-half hour scenic bus ride to the Wetherill visitors' area, where they transfer to minibus trains that take

Long House at Wetherill Mesa, one of the largest cliff dwellings at Mesa Verde

Long House, open dance plaza with large fire pit and foot drums in the foreground

groups to the head of the trail to **Long House,** * one of the two ruins open to the public.

The trail to Long House is a steep, one-mile round trip that is not accessible to persons in wheelchairs or to those suffering from heart or respiratory conditions. Park rangers take groups on tours through Long House, the second largest ruin in Mesa Verde National Park. This cliff ruin had 150 rooms and 21 kivas and housed 150 to 175 persons. It was two stories high in some places and had small storage rooms on a narrow ledge above the main structure. The outstanding characteristic of Long House is the central plaza, which has some of the features of a great kiva and probably served some of the same functions. It has a large central fire pit flanked by two foot drums and benches around three sides that were used by Anasazi as they watched the ceremonies. The only structure similar to this is the open plaza at Sun Temple on Chapin Mesa.

Step House, * the other ruin on Wetherill Mesa open to the public, is reached by a one-half-mile trail that heads near the Wetherill visitors' area. This ruin was named for a long flight of stone steps built by the Anasazi to enter the structure from above. This site is unique because visitors may view two separate periods of occupation: Basketmaker II (A.D. 626) and Pueblo II (A.D. 1226).

Partially restored pithouse from the Basket-maker occupation at
Step House, Mesa Verde

The former period is represented by the remains of four excavated
pithouses and the latter by a masonry pueblo that housed thirty to
forty persons. One of these pithouses has been restored to show
how it would have appeared in the seventh century. On a wall of
the pueblo is a group of petroglyphs of animal, human, and geometric forms. One kiva still shows some of the many layers of
plaster on its walls.

Both Long House and Step House are in areas where the surroundings show little signs of the disturbance of modern man that
mar some of the beauty of sites on Chapin Mesa. This makes the
new area a good place to visit for those who can hike the short but
steep trails.

Other major excavated cliff sites on Wetherill Mesa with the
number of rooms in parentheses are: **Mug House** (ninety-four),
Kodak House (sixty), **Jug House** (seventy-five), **Ruin 16** (fifty), and
Ruin 20½ (fifty). Mug House is excavated and prepared for visitors
and will be open as soon as the trail is completed. The three major
excavated mesatop sites on Wetherill Mesa are known as **Big
Juniper House, Badger Community,** and **Two Raven House.**

Yucca House was first described by W. H. Holmes in 1877. It
is 8.5 miles southwest of Cortez, Colorado. The ten acres on which

the site is located were donated by Henry Van Kleek for the monument. The structure was composed of two house units. The upper, larger section had terraced structures three or four stories in height. The smaller, lower section was a long row of one- or two-story rooms facing a walled compound. There are a number of circular depressions, indicating the probable presence of kivas. The ruin is built of roughly dressed limestone laid in mortar. The site has not been excavated, so little is known concerning the inhabitants or their culture. It is estimated that Yucca House was inhabited circa A.D. 1000 to 1300. The site consists of a low mound with faint evidences of walls. Hopefully it will be excavated and restored in future years.

Southwest of Mesa Verde National Park in the Mancos River canyon is **Ute Mountain Ute Tribal Park.*** From Cortez, take U.S. Highway No. 666 about twenty-three miles south, turn east at the tribal gas station on a gravel road, and follow the signs up Mancos Canyon. This park, owned and operated by the Ute Mountain Ute Indian Tribe, has many surface ruins in addition to a large number of cliff dwellings. Some of these sites have been excavated and restored for visitors. Excavation was done under the direction of Dave Breternitz in the early 1970s.

Tree House* is a cliff dwelling of twenty-seven rooms and three kivas. It can be reached only from a ladder that extends down from the rim of the cliff. This ruin is named for a large Douglas fir that grows in front of it from the canyon below. At one end of this ruin is a three-story tower.

At a place called Kiva Point is a group of ruins that includes what may be several great kivas. A pueblo known as **5MTUMR 2346** is three miles from Kiva Point and was excavated by Breternitz. This structure has tree-ring dates of A.D. 1000 to 1250 and contained twenty-five rooms. Broken human bones indicate that cannibalism was practiced by the inhabitants of this site. This is one of the very few documented cases of this practice in the Southwest.

Other cliff dwellings, located in Lion and Johnson canyons, are: **Eagles Nest*** (thirteen rooms and one kiva on a high ledge, and five rooms at the base of the cliff); **She House** (twelve rooms and one kiva); **Hoy House*** (sixty rooms and four kivas); **Fortified House** (twenty-four rooms and one kiva); and **Lion House** (forty-six rooms and six kivas). The masonry in these cliff dwellings is similar to that in Mesa Verde to the north, but the dwellings are smaller and were occupied somewhat later. The sites in this park range from Basketmaker III to Pueblo III times. Lion House and Hoy House were occupied from A.D. 1140 to 1240 but were abandoned from A.D. 1160 to 1195.

The Ute Mountain Ute Indian Tribe is developing camping and other facilities in the park, and there is fishing in the Mancos River. When this area becomes better developed, it will be an excellent place to vacation and view the ruins. Current information concerning Ute Mountain Ute Tribal Park may be obtained at the Ute pottery factory on the west side of U.S. Highway 666, south of Cortez, Colorado. Small groups of less than fifteen persons who wish a preview of the park may make arrangements for a guide by writing to the Ute Mountain Tribal Park, General Delivery, Towaoc, Colorado 81334.

Wallace Ruin is located in a small valley approximately 4.2 miles east of Cortez. It is part of the Lakeview Ruin Group, which also includes **Haney Ruin** to the south and **Ida Jean Ruin** to the southeast. Wallace Ruin is a multiroomed, two-storied pueblo. It was built in the shape of a "U" and was constructed of stone masonry. This site was occupied during Pueblo II and III times and was excavated by Bruce Bradley from 1969 to 1975.

Another interesting site in this area is **Site 33, Johnson Canyon,** southeast of Mesa Verde National Park. It is located on the mesa between Johnson and Greasewood canyons. This is a large, multicomponent site composed of three Pueblo I structures, associated pithouses, and a great kiva. There is also a late Pueblo III (Mesa Verde) structure of fourteen rooms built around an enclosed kiva. This site was excavated by Earl Morris in the 1930s. Permission to visit this ruin and others on the Southern Ute Indian Reservation should be sought at the tribal headquarters in Ignacio, Colorado.

Map 15
Prehistoric Ruins of the Chaco Canyon Area

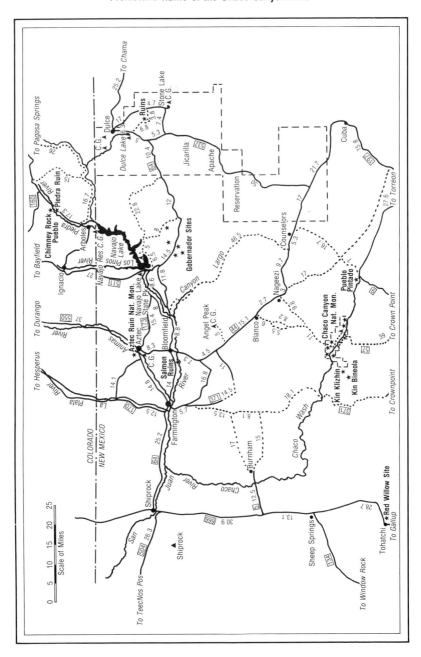

XIV

Chaco Canyon Area

This area encompasses the drainage of the Chaco River, an intermittent southern tributary of the San Juan River; the country to the east and north around Farmington, New Mexico; and the Piedra River valley of southern Colorado. It contains some extensive and well-preserved pueblo ruins of the Anasazi culture. The locations of the major ruins in this area are shown on Map #15.

The vicinity of Aztec, New Mexico, can be visited from a motel in the area or by camping nearby. Two outstanding sites in this area are the Salmon Ruins near Bloomfield, New Mexico, and Aztec Ruin at Aztec. Salmon Ruin is presently under excavation by the San Juan County Archeological Research Center and has a good museum with exhibits of artifacts found at this site. Aztec Ruin is an easily visited site and includes the only completely restored great kiva in existence.

Chaco Canyon National Monument contains an outstanding concentration of major pueblo ruins and is considered by some to be the most interesting prehistoric area in the United States. Aztec, Salmon, and Chaco Canyon are near the top of the list for ruins buffs and fortunately can be visited in one trip. No lodging is available at or near Chaco Canyon National Monument, and because there is so much to see, it is recommended that visitors plan to camp for at least one night at the monument. The campground is usually uncrowded, and spending a night or two among these great stone cities is a unique experience. A walk through one of these ruins at sunset was a high point in my many years of camping near prehistoric sites. Weatherwise, spring and fall are the best times to visit this area, but infrequent downpours may make the roads to Chaco impassable for short periods. The extra effort it may take to reach Chaco Canyon will be well repaid, however.

Aztec Ruins National Monument* is one mile north of the town of Aztec, New Mexico, on U.S. Highway No. 550 in the Animas River Valley. The address is Route 1, Box 101, Aztec Ruins, New Mexico 87410.

Aztec Ruin is a quadrangle of stone masonry rooms, three stories high at some points. The main ruin is 360 feet by 275 feet

Aztec Ruins National Monument, New Mexico

and contained a total of 500 rooms. It had an estimated population of 450. The total area of the site, including some outlying structures, is twenty-five acres. The ruin includes twelve or more small kivas and one great kiva that was restored by Earl Morris in 1934. The great kiva is the outstanding feature at Aztec, and standing in this impressive building gives you an idea of what it must have been like during the ancient ceremonials.

Great Kiva restored by Earl H. Morris in 1934, Aztec Ruins
National Monument

Interior of restored Great Kiva at Aztec National Monument,
Aztec, New Mexico

169

Kiva with roof beams in place, note differences in masonry from several building periods, Aztec National Monument

The masonry at Aztec is remarkably well done and shows influences from both the Mesa Verde people to the north and the Chacoans to the south. An unusual decorative band of green sandstone runs along one outer wall.

Adjacent to the main ruin is an excavated, circular structure known as the **Hubbard Tri-Wall Site.** Also at the monument are two other unexcavated ruins named **East Ruin** and **Earl Morris Ruin.**

There is a self-guided trail through the main ruin and to the Hubbard Tri-Wall. Aztec was occupied intermittently from A.D. 1100 to 1285 and was excavated by Earl Morris from 1916 to 1921. The monument has a visitors' center with a museum containing pottery and other items found at Aztec. The monument is open year-round from 8:00 AM to 5:00 PM except December 25 and January 1. Lodging and camping are available nearby at Aztec. This monument is a good place to visit because it is compact, but most of it is not accessible to wheelchairs. The museum, visitors' center, restrooms, and plaza can be reached in a wheelchair, and part of the self-guided trail can be traveled with assistance.

Salmon Ruins* (Chaco 8:7GP) is a few miles south of Aztec National Monument. It is one mile west of Bloomfield, New

Salmon Ruins, Bloomfield, New Mexico

Mexico, on U.S. Highway 64 and is situated on the second bench above the San Juan River.

This is a very large "C"-shaped pueblo, 500 feet by 200 feet and containing 600 to 750 rooms. It was three stories high in some places. There is a large kiva in the courtyard and other small kivas within the main structure. The original portion was built in the late 1000s or early 1100s of Chaco-style masonry and occupied for less than 100 years. It was abandoned and then reoccupied by Mesa Verde people. This history is very similar to that of Aztec Ruin.

Salmon Ruin is owned and is being excavated by the San Juan County Archeological Research Center. Large crews of students have been working here during the summer months since 1972 under the direction of Dr. Cynthia Irwin–Williams of Eastern New Mexico University. The research center maintains a good museum with a slide show and a research library at the site. There is a self-guided tour of the ruin, and much of the site will be accessible to persons in wheelchairs when it is fully developed. The center and the ruin are open daily during the summer months.

This site also contains the early twentieth-century homestead of George Salmon, who owned and protected this site for many years. Fortunately, Salmon did not permit pothunting at his ruin.

Large masonry rooms under excavation at Salmon Ruins

Therefore, it is one of the few large sites that has remained undisturbed and that has therefore retained its scientific value.

There are motels at Bloomfield and campgrounds near Aztec and at Navajo Lake, twenty-seven miles to the northeast. Salmon Ruin is not well-known outside this area, but it is a very interesting ruin and will become even more attractive as it is excavated and more fully developed.

Chaco Canyon National Monument* is one of the outstanding prehistoric site areas in the United States. It is located in northwestern New Mexico, south of Farmington and northeast of Gallup. To reach it from the north, turn off New Mexico Highway No. 44 at Blanco Trading Post onto New Mexico Highway No. 57, a gravel road. It is twenty-three miles to the monument entrance and seven more miles to the visitors' center in the canyon. This road is fine in good weather, but it is slippery when wet. To reach Chaco from the south, turn north on New Mexico Highway No. 57 from Interstate 40 at Thoreau, and drive north sixty-four miles to the south entrance. The visitors' center is about two miles farther. There are about twenty-one miles of gravel road along this route. The superintendent's address is P.O. Box 156, Bloomfield, New Mexico 87413.

The monument is roughly two by nine miles in size. The climate is arid, and the region is isolated from any centers of population. Chaco Canyon has eighteen major ruins and hundreds of smaller ones. The prehistoric population may have reached 5,000.

There are self-guided trails at the three ruins of **Pueblo Bonito,** * **Chettro Kettle,** * and **Casa Rinconada.** * Pueblo Bonito, the largest ruin, contained 800 rooms and 32 kivas and was occupied from A.D. 828 to 1126. Bonito is quite well preserved and is built of some of the best stone masonry in the Southwest. In January 1941, a section of the nearby canyon wall collapsed, destroying part of the rear wall and some rooms at Bonito. The rim of the canyon provides a good spot from which to photograph this ruin.

In addition to the three ruins mentioned above, the other major ruins in the main section of Chaco Canyon are **Penasco Blanco,** * **Casa Chiquita,** * **Kin Kletso,** * **Pueblo Alto,** * **Pueblo del Arroyo,** * **Tsin Kletzin,** * **Hungo Pavie,** * **Kin Nahasbas,** * **Una Vida,** * and **Wijiji.** * Hikers will be interested in these ruins, which can be reached only by short hikes from the road in the canyon floor. Wijiji can be reached by an easy two-mile hike up the canyon

Campground in Gallo Canyon, Chaco Canyon National Monument, New Mexico

173

Pueblo Bonito, Chaco Canyon, rubble of huge rockfall in background

Excavated rooms and high back wall of very fine masonry at Chettro Kettle, Chaco Canyon

Three excavated kivas at Pueblo del Arroyo, Chaco Canyon
National Monument

from the campground. On the mesatop above Casa Rinconada is
Tsin Kletzin, located at the end of a two-mile trail that traverses
some sand dunes. Two and one-half miles from the point where the
road north leaves the canyon is the ruin of Penasco Blanco. This
trail goes down the canyon, then climbs to the top of the mesa on
the south side. Permits are required for all backcountry travel.

Four detached sections of the monument are located seven to
forty miles from the main area. The names of the ruins at the detached sections are **Kin Biniola,** to the southwest; **Kin Klizhin,** to
the west; **Pueblo Pintado,** to the southeast; and **Kin Ya-ah,** to the
south. Visitors should obtain permission and directions from the
ranger at the monument headquarters to visit the outlying sections.

The sites at Chaco Canyon cover the range of time from
Basketmaker II to Pueblo III. **Shabik'eshchee Village*** (A.D. 950),
in the southeastern corner of the monument, is a noted Basketmaker pithouse village. It is on top of the mesa that forms the
southern wall of Chaco Canyon. This small village consisted of
eighteen houses, a small court, a large ceremonial structure or kiva,
and forty-eight storage bins. The houses were circular, oval, or rectangular in shape and were formed of excavated lower portions

175

A short hike up the canyon from the campground are the ruins of Wijiji, Chaco Canyon

A Navajo crew restoring masonry walls at Wijiji, Chaco Canyon National Monument

roofed with poles, brush, and plaster. The earth walls of the excavation were plastered, and in some of these pithouses, the excavated walls were lined with large stone slabs. Near most of the houses were round or oval pits in which corn was stored. The large circular ceremonial structure was near the center of the village and appears to have been the forerunner of the great kivas in the Pueblo III villages on the canyon floor. There is little to see at Shabik'eshchee today, but it is an interesting hike to this site for the avid ruin visitor who wants to hike beyond Wijiji.

Chaco Canyon sites were excavated by George H. Pepper in 1896, Neil J. Judd in 1921 to 1927, and the personnel of several institutions in recent years. Currently, the Chaco Research Center at the University of New Mexico is conducting extensive studies here. Recent research has shown the presence of long, very straight, prehistoric "roads" from one site to another. The use of these roads is not known. Study indicates that the Chacoans had active trade with other regions, including the people to the south in Mexico.

The visitors' center at Chaco Canyon has some exhibits of artifacts, and the monument is open year-round. The staff is very helpful in answering questions and giving directions. The monument has a campground with a restroom and drinking water but no firewood or hookups. No food, gasoline, or other supplies are available at Chaco Canyon, so visitors should make sure that they are well supplied before venturing here. Persons in wheelchairs can see some of the major ruins with assistance.

A recent book by Douglas and Barbara Anderson gives a good introduction and color photographs of this outstanding prehistoric site area (Anderson, 1976).

Red Willow Site (LA 4470) was excavated in a salvage project by Stewart Peckham in 1959. It is located on the Navajo Reservation southeast of Tohatchi, New Mexico, on U.S. Highway No. 666. The pueblo is on a small promontory, about midway down the steep, talus-strewn slope of the mesa. A bi-wall structure is situated at the very edge of the top of the mesa, about sixty feet above the pueblo. This site is divided into two parts: a masonry pueblo of about twenty rooms, and a detached bi-wall structure. The bi-wall was dated at A.D. 1125 to 1175. There is a campground at Red Rocks State Park, east of Gallup, New Mexico.

The eastern part of this area is not well-known, but it is very scenic and has some interesting sites. The region encompasses northern New Mexico and southern Colorado in the valley of the Piedra River and Gobernador Canyon to the south. This is the ancestral home of the Navajo people, where they lived prior to their move to their present location to the southwest.

Good camping and fishing are available in this locality, and it is not heavily visited. Navajo Lake at the confluence of the Piedra and Los Pinos rivers has camping, boating, and fishing. Some of the best trout fishing in New Mexico is on the San Juan River below Navajo Dam. To the east is the Jicarilla Apache Indian Reservation with developed recreational areas at several lakes and some stream fishing. There are a few ruins on this reservation. Information and permission to visit the sites may be obtained at the tribal headquarters in Dulce, New Mexico.

The Cumbres and Toltec Railroad is a narrow-gauge sight-seeing line that runs between Chama, New Mexico, and Antonito, Colorado, through some beautiful, wild country.

In **Gobernador Canyon** and its side canyons are a number of Navajo period sites.

Site No. 3 (LA 1869) is located on the south rim of Canyon San Rafael. It is a masonry pueblo of thirteen rooms and eight hogans and is enclosed by a stone wall. **Site No. 4** (LA 1871) is situated on an isolated pinnacle of rock in Canyon San Rafael, about one-half mile southwest of Site No. 3. This site consists of a masonry pueblo of twelve ground-floor rooms, an entrance labyrinth, and two hogans in a plaza. **Site No. 6** is located north of Gobernador Canyon on the north rim of a side canyon that enters Canyon Francis from the west. This site is composed of a forty-room masonry pueblo with a court and a three-story tower.

These sites were surveyed in 1915 by Earl Morris and described by Roy Carlson in 1965. (The site numbers here are from Carlson's report.) These sites are not easy to find, and it is advisable to obtain local directions or a guide. There are campgrounds to the west at Navajo Lake State Park or east on the Jicarilla Reservation.

Piedra Ruin (Colo:B:15:1 GP) is located on Stollsteimer Mesa in Piedra Valley. This site is composed of six small house groups, each with an accompanying kiva or depression. Unit C-3 is a four-room house group at this Pueblo I village. Frank H. H. Roberts excavated part of this site in 1928. The single tree-ring date for Unit C-3 is A.D. 774. There are several good places to camp and fish in this vicinity.

Chimney Rock Mesa District* is located in Archuleta County, Colorado, north of the small town of Arboles in the Piedra River valley. The site groups are situated southwest of the twin pinnacles of Chimney Rock, for which the ruins are named. The sites are east of the Piedra River between two tributaries named Stollsteimer Creek and Devil's Creek. An access road leaves Colorado Highway No. 151 about five to six miles southwest of its junction with U.S. Highway No. 160. Seventy-four sites are included in the seven named site groups, and seventeen isolated sites were found in the area surveyed.

The names and some major characteristics of these groups are as follows. **High Mesa Group*** is the largest, highest in elevation (7,600 feet), and probably of the most interest to visitors. It contains a tight cluster of sixteen sites, several of which have been excavated and restored. The three most notable are **Chimney Rock Pueblo*** (5AA83), the **Guard House*** (5AA84), and **Parking Lot Site*** (5AA86).

Chimney Rock Pueblo is the best known and most impressive of these structures. It is a Chaco-style sandstone masonry pueblo and differs significantly in architecture from all of the other sites in this district. It probably was built by a group of immigrants from the Chaco Canyon area who resided contemporaneously with the indigenous Chimney Rock people. This pueblo contained thirty-five ground-floor rooms and two kivas enclosed in rectangular room blocks. The total number of rooms is estimated at fifty. The east kiva has been excavated and is a typical Chaco-type kiva except that it lacks the usual sipapu and deflector in the floor. The pueblo is situated on a high mesa 1,000 feet above the valley floor. There is a plaza south of the pueblo and a partially enclosed court to the east. A trash deposit is situated at the base of the cliff along the north side of the building.

The site group known as **Southern Piedra** has six architectural sites, including small pueblos and great kivas. **Northern Piedra Group** is second to the High Mesa Group in number of structures. It has fourteen sites, containing seventy buildings that include three single units, two multiple units, seven villages, twenty-one masonry pueblos, six pithouses or small kivas, and seven great kivas.

The four other unexcavated ruin groups are known as East Slope, Stollsteimer, Ravine and Pyramid.

With the exception of the High Mesa Group, nearly all of the sites in this district are unexcavated. The types of structures have been deduced from the shapes of the surface evidence and from testing. The population of all the sites in the above-named groups, plus the seventeen isolated sites in the Chimney Rock District, has been estimated at 1,215 to 2,025 persons.

The initial excavations at Chimney Rock were conducted by Jean A. Jeancon for the Colorado State Historical Society in 1921, and in 1922, Frank H. H. Roberts directed the dig for the historical society. No excavation was done for fifty years, and some damage was done by pothunters during this period. In 1970 to 1972, Frank Eddy directed excavations and stabilization for the University of Colorado and the U.S. Forest Service.

The four dwellings excavated in 1970 to 1972 are all Anasazi Pueblo II sites dating from A.D. 925 to 1125. Chimney Rock Pueblo was occupied for fifty years, from A.D. 1076 to 1125. For persons seeking more information concerning Chimney Rock, Frank Eddy's report, published by the Colorado Archeological Society in 1977, is recommended.

In 1980, this area was not yet open to the public, but when the forest service completes the visitors' facilities, the sites will provide a valuable addition to the public understanding of the prehistory of the Chimney Rock area. The Ute Campground and Capote Lake Recreation Area owned by the Southern Ute Indian Tribe provide good camping a few miles northeast of Chimney Rock.

XV

Conclusion

This guide provides information concerning more than 200 prehistoric sites and ruins in the Southwest. Over 150 of these are protected and recommended for visits; others may be seen with permission of the private landowners or federal land managers. Sites recommended for visits are marked by an asterisk in the text and in the index.

Ruins can be appreciated in one or more ways, three of which might be termed scientific, aesthetic, and spiritual. Unfortunately, only the objective physical characteristics of the ancient sites can be adequately described through words and pictures. Therefore, the appreciation on the other two levels must come, if at all, from personally experiencing the site and its surroundings. Whether or not the beauty and spirituality of ancient man and his works are experienced seems to depend upon the interaction of the environmental setting and the "mind set" of the individual visitors.

It is my experience that camping at or near a site increases the probability of a deep personal experience. This is true because the quiet and muted light of sunset and dawn are more conducive to contemplation than the crowds and glare of midday. The quiet and shadows of a sunset at Kiet Siel, dawn breaking over Pueblo Bonito, or Lowry Ruin bathed in moonlight encourage a feeling of oneness with the ancient inhabitants. Whether you are interested in the science of archeology, prehistoric ruins as art, or are seeking a spiritual experience, my efforts will be well repaid if this guide has assisted you.

Bibliography

Ambler, J. Richard. *Anasazi.* Museum of Northern Arizona, Flagstaff, Arizona, 1977. $4.25.

Anderson, Douglas and Barbara. *Chaco Canyon.* Popular Series No. 17, Southwest Parks and Monuments Association, Globe, Arizona, 1976. $3.00.

Bandelier, Adolph F. *The Delightmakers.* Originally published in 1890. Harcourt Brace Jovanovich, Inc., 1976. $4.25.

Barnes, Fran A., and Pendleton, Michaelene. *Canyon Country Prehistoric Indians.* Wasatch Publishers, Inc., Salt Lake City, 1979. $5.95.

Barnett, Franklin. *Crooked Arrow.* Beaumaris Books, Tempe, Arizona, 1977. $4.95.

Bohn, Dave, and Jett, Stephen. *House of Three Turkeys: Anasazi Redoubt.* Capra Press, Santa Barbara, California, 1977. $3.95.

Bradley, Zorro A. *Canyon de Chelly: The Story of Its Ruins and Canyons.* National Park Service, Department of Interior, Washington, D.C., 1973. $1.25.

Brew, J. O. "Archaeology of Alkali Ridge, Southeastern Utah." *Papers of the Peabody Museum of Archaeology and Ethnology,* Harvard University, Cambridge, Massachusetts, Vol. 21, 1946.

Brody, J. J. *Mimbres Painted Pottery.* School of American Research, Santa Fe, New Mexico, 1977. $22.50.

Butcher, Devereux. *Exploring Our Prehistoric Indian Ruins.* National Parks Association, Washington, D.C., 1950.

Castelton, Kenneth B. *Petroglyphs and Pictographs of Utah, Vol. 2.* Utah Museum of Natural History, Salt Lake City, 1979. $15.00.

Colton, Harold S. "The Sinagua: A Summary of the Archaeology of the Region of Northern Arizona." *Museum of Northern Arizona Bulletin 22*, Flagstaff, Arizona, 1946. (out of print)

Corbett, John M. *Aztec Ruins National Monument*. National Park Service Historical Handbook Series No. 36, Washington, D.C., 1962. $0.50.

Current, William, and Scully, Vincent. *Pueblo Architecture of the Southwest*. Amon Carter Museum of Western Art, University of Texas Press, Austin, 1971. $12.50.

Dutton, Bertha P. *Let's Explore Indian Villages: Past and Present. No. 1—Santa Fe Area*. Museum of New Mexico Press, Santa Fe, 1962. $1.00.

Eddy, Frank W. "Archaeological Investigations at Chimney Rock Mesa: 1970-1972." *Memoirs of the Colorado Archaeological Society*, No. 1, Boulder, Colorado, 1977. $6.95.

Folsom, Franklin. *America's Ancient Treasures: Guide to Archaeological Sites and Museums*. Rand McNally, New York, 1971. $2.95.

Grant, Campbell. *Canyon de Chelly: Its People and Rock Art*. University of Arizona Press, Tucson, 1978. $19.50.

Haury, Emil W. *The Hohokam: Desert Farmers and Craftsmen, Excavations at Snaketown, 1964-1965*. University of Arizona, Tucson, 1974. $19.50.

Hewett, Edgar L. *Pajarito Plateau and Its Ancient People*. University of New Mexico Press, Albuquerque, New Mexico, 1938. (out of print)

Hibben, Frank C. *Kiva Art of the Anasazi at Pottery Mound*. KC Publications, Las Vegas, Nevada, 1975. $35.00.

Hoard, Dorothy. *A Hiker's Guide to Bandelier National Monument*. Adobe Press, Albuquerque, New Mexico, 1978. $3.75.

Hightower, Jamake. *Fodor's Indian America*. David McKay Company, Inc., New York, 1975. $10.95.

Horgan, Paul. *Great River: The Rio Grande, Vol. I, Indians and Spain*. Minerva Press, 1954. $2.95.

Jackson, Earl. *Your National Park Service in the Southwest*. 3rd Edition, Revised. Southwest Parks and Monuments Association, Globe, Arizona, 1976. $6.00.

Jennings, Jesse D. *Glen Canyon: A Summary*. University of Utah Anthropological Papers No. 81. Salt Lake City, Utah, 1966. $8.00.

King, Patrick. *Pueblo Indian Religious Architecture.* Published by the author. P.O. Box 8451, Salt Lake City, Utah. 1975. $1.75.

Lister, Florence C., and Lister, Robert H. *Earl Morris and Southwestern Archaeology.* University of New Mexico Press, Albuquerque, New Mexico, 1968. $7.95.

Lohman, S. W. *The Geologic Story of Canyonlands National Park.* Geological Survey Bulletin 1327. U.S. Government Printing Office, Washington, D.C., 1974. $2.65.

Lowenkopf, Anne N., and Katz, Michael W. *Camping with the Indians.* Sherbourne Press, Inc., Los Angeles, California, 1974. $4.95.

Marquis, Arnold. *A Guide to America's Indians: Ceremonials, Reservations, and Museums.* University of Oklahoma Press, Norman, 1974. $4.95.

Martin, Paul S., and Plog, Fred. *The Archaeology of Arizona: A Study of the Southwest Region.* Doubleday, Natural History Press, Garden City, New York, 1973. $17.50.

McFarland, Elizabeth. *Forever Frontier: The Gila Cliff Dwellings.* University of New Mexico Press, Albuquerque, 1967. $2.00.

McNitt, Frank. *Richard Wetherill: Anasazi.* University of New Mexico Press, Albuquerque, 1957. $4.50.

Muench, David, and Pike, Donald. *Anasazi: Ancient People of the Rock.* American West Publishing Company, Palo Alto, California, 1974. $16.95.

Noble, David. *Ancient Ruins of the Southwest.* Northland Press, Flagstaff, Arizona, 1981. $8.95.

Rohn, Arthur H. *Cultural Change and Continuity on Chapin Mesa.* University of Kansas Press, Lawrence, Kansas, 1977. $16.00.

Schroeder, Albert H., and Hastings, Homer F. *Montezuma Castle National Monument.* National Park Service Historical Handbook Series No. 27, Washington, D.C., 1961. $0.65.

Schwartz, Douglas W., Marshall, Michael P., and Kepp, Jane. *Archaeology of the Grand Canyon: The Bright Angel Site.* Grand Canyon Archaeological Series, Vol. 1. School of American Research, Santa Fe, New Mexico, 1979. $4.95.

Smith, Watson, Woodbury, Richard B., and Woodbury, Natalie, F. S. *The Excavation of Hawikuh by Frederick W. Hodge, 1917-1923.* Contributions of the Museum of the American Indian, Heye Foundation, Vol. 20, New York, 1966.

Steen, Charlie, Pierson, L. M., Bohrer, V. L., and Kent, Kate P. *Archaeological Studies in Tonto National Monument.* Technical Series Vol. 2, Southwest Monuments Association, Globe, Arizona, 1962. $4.50.

Sunset Books. *Southwest Indian Country.* Lane Books, Menlo Park, California, 1977. $1.95.

Ward, Albert E. "Inscription House: Two Research Reports." *Museum of Northern Arizona, Technical Series No. 16.* Museum of Arizona, Flagstaff, Arizona, 1975. $4.50.

Watson, Don. *Indians of the Mesa Verde.* Mesa Verde Museum Association, Mesa Verde National Park, Colorado, 1961. $6.50.

Wheat, Joe Ben. *Prehistoric People of the Northern Southwest.* Bulletin No. 12, Grand Canyon Natural History Association, Northland Press, Flagstaff, Arizona, 1953. $2.00.

Wheat, Joe Ben. *Mogollon Culture Prior to A.D. 1000.* American Anthropological Association, Vol. 57, No. 2, Part 3, Memoir 82, 1955.

Wing, Kittridge A. *Bandelier National Monument, New Mexico.* National Park Service Historical Handbook Series No. 23, Washington, D.C., 1955. $0.50.

Winter, Joseph C. "Hovenweep 1974." *Archaeological Report No. 1.* Anthropology Department, San Jose State University, San Jose, California, 1975.

Appendix I

PUBLIC LAW 96-95—Oct. 31, 1979

An Act

To protect archaeological resources on public lands and Indian lands and for other purposes.

Short Title

Section 1. This Act may be cited as the "Archaeological Resources Protection Act of 1979."

Findings and Purpose

Section 2.(a) The Congress finds that—

(1) archaeological resources on public lands and Indian lands are an accessible and irreplaceable part of the Nation's heritage;

(2) these resources are increasingly endangered because of their commercial attractiveness;

(3) existing Federal laws do not provide adequate protection to prevent the loss and destruction of these archaeological resources and sites resulting from uncontrolled excavation and pillage and;

(4) there is a wealth of archaeological information which has been legally obtained by private individuals for noncommercial purposes and which could voluntarily be made available to professional archaeologists and institutions.

(b) The purpose of this Act is to secure, for the present and future benefit of the American people, the protection of archaeological resources and sites which are on public lands and Indian lands, and to foster increased cooperation and exchange of information between governmental authorities, the professional archaeological community, and private individuals having collections of archaeological resources and data which were obtained before the date of the enactment of this Act.

Definitions

Section 3. As used in this Act—

(1) the term "archaeological resources" means any material remains of past human life or activities which are of archaeological interest, as determined under uniform regulations promulgated pursuant to this Act. Such regulations containing such determination shall include, but not be limited to: pottery, basketry, bottles, weapons, weapon projectiles, tools, structures, or portions of structures, pit houses, rock paintings, rock carvings, intaglios, graves, human skeletal materials, or any portion or piece of any of the foregoing items. Nonfossilized and fossilized paleontological specimens, or any portion or piece thereof, shall not be considered archaeological resources under the regulations of this paragraph, unless found in an archaeological context. No item shall be treated as an archaeological resource under regulations under this paragraph unless such item is at least 100 years of age.

(2) the term "Federal land manager" means with respect to any public lands, the Secretary of the department, or the head of any other agency or instrumentality of the United States, having primary management authority over such lands. In the case of any public lands or Indian lands with respect to which no department, agency or instrumentality has primary management authority, such term means the Secretary of the Interior. If the Secretary of the Interior consents, the responsibilities (in whole or in part) under this Act of the Secretary of any department (other than the Department of the Interior) or the head of any such agency or instrumentality may be delegated to the Secretary of the Interior with respect any land managed by such other Secretary or agency head, and in any such case, the term "federal land manager" means the Secretary of the Interior.

(3) The term "public lands" means—

    (A) lands which are owned and administered by the United States as part of—
        (i) the national park system
        (ii) the national wildlife refuge system, or
        (iii) the national forest system; and
    (B) all other lands the fee title to which is held by the

United States, other than those lands on the Outer Continental Shelf and lands which are under jurisdiction of the Smithsonian Institution;

(4) The term "Indian lands" means lands of Indian tribes, or Indian individuals, which are either held in trust by the United States or subject to a restriction against alienation imposed by the United States, except for any subsurface interests in lands not owned or controlled by an Indian tribe or an Indian individual.

(5) The term "Indian tribe" means any Indian tribe, band, nation, or other organized group or community, including any Alaska Native village or regional or village corporation as defined in, or established pursuant to, the Alaska Native Claims Settlement Act (85 Stat. 688).

(6) The term "person" means any individual, corporation, partnership, trust, institution, association, or any other private entity or any officer, employee, agent, department, or instrumentality of the United States, of any Indian tribe, or any State or political subdivision thereof.

(7) The term "State" means any of the fifty states, the District of Columbia, Puerto Rico, Guam, and the Virgin Islands.

Excavation and Removal

Section 4.(a) Any person may apply to the Federal land manager for a permit to excavate or remove any archaeological resource located on public lands or Indian Lands and to carry out activities associated with such excavation or removal. The application shall be required, under this Act, to contain such information as the Federal land manager deems necessary, including information concerning the time, scope, and location and specific purpose of the proposed work.

(b) A permit may be issued pursuant to an application under subsection (a) if the Federal land manager determines, pursuant to uniform regulations under this Act, that—

(1) the applicant is qualified, to carry out the permitted activity,

(2) the activity is undertaken for the purpose of furthering archaeological knowledge in the public interest,

(3) the archaeological resources which are excavated or removed from public lands will remain the property of the United States, and such resources and copies of associated archaeological records and data will be preserved by a suitable university, museum, or other scientific or educational institution, and

(4) the activity pursuant to this permit is not inconsistent with any management plan applicable to the public lands concerned.

(c) If a permit issued under the section may result in harm to, or destruction of, any religious or cultural site, as determined by the federal land manager, before issuing such permit, the Federal land manager shall notify any Indian tribe which may consider the site as having religious or cultural importance. Such notice shall not be deemed a disclosure to the public for the purpose of section 9.

(d) Any permit under this section shall contain such terms and conditions, pursuant to uniform regulations promulgated under this Act, as the Federal land manager concerned deems necessary to carry out the purposes of this Act.

(e) Each permit under this section shall identify the individual who shall be responsible for carrying out the terms and conditions of the permit and for otherwise complying with this Act and other law applicable to the permitted activity.

(f) Any permit issued under this section may be suspended by the Federal land manager upon his determination that the permittee has violated any provision of subsection (a), (b), or (c), or section 6. Any such permit may be revoked by such Federal land manager upon assessment of a civil penalty under section 7 against the permittee or upon the permittee's conviction under section 6.

(g) (1) No permit shall be required under this section or under the Act of June 8, 1906 (16 U.S.C. 431), for the excavation or removal by any Indian tribe or member thereof of any archaeological resource located on Indian lands of such Indian tribe, except that in the absence of tribal law regulating the excavation or removal of archaeological resources on Indian lands, an individual tribe member shall be required to obtain a permit under this section.

(2) In the case of any permits for excavation or removal of any archaeological resource located on Indian lands, the permit may be granted only after obtaining the consent of the Indian or Indian tribe owning or having jurisdiction over such lands. The permit shall include such terms and conditions as may be requested by such Indian or Indian tribe.

(h) (1) No permit or other permission shall be required under the Act of June 8, 1906 (16 U.S.C. 431-433) for any activity for which a permit is issued under this section.

(2) Any permit issued under the Act of June 8, 1906, shall remain in effect according to its terms and conditions following the

enactment of this Act shall be required to carry out any activity under a permit issued under the Act of June 8, 1906, before the date of the enactment of this Act which remains in effect as provided in this paragraph, and nothing in this Act shall modify or affect any such permit.

(i) Issuance of a permit in accordance with this section and applicable regulations shall not require compliance with section 106 of the Act of October 15, 1966 (80 Stat. 817, 16 U.S.C. 470f).

(j) Upon the written request of the Governor of any state, the Federal land manager shall issue a permit, subject to the provisions of subsections (b)(3), (b)(4), (c), (3), (f), (g), (h), and (i) of this section for the purpose of conducting archaeological research, excavation, removal, and curation on behalf of the State or its educational institutions, to such Governor or to such designee as the Governor deems qualified to carry out the intent of this Act.

Custody of Resources

Section 5. The Secretary of the Interior may promulgate regulations providing for—

(1) the exchange, where appropriate, between suitable universities, museums, or other scientific or educational institutions, or archaeological resources removed from public lands and Indian lands pursuant to this Act, and

(2) the ultimate disposition of such resources and other resources removed pursuant to the Act of June 27, 1960 (16 U.S.C. 469-469c) or the Act of June 8, 1906 (16 U.S.C. 431-433). Any exchange or ultimate distribution under such regulation of archaeological resources excavated or removed from Indian lands shall be subject to the consent of the Indian or Indian tribe which owns or has jurisdiction over such lands. Following promulgation of regulations under this section, notwithstanding any other provision of law, such regulations shall govern the disposition of archaeological resources removed from public lands and Indian lands pursuant to this Act.

Prohibited Acts and Criminal Penalties

Section 6.(a) No person may excavate, remove, damage, or otherwise alter or deface any archaeological resource located on public lands or Indian lands unless such activity is pursuant to a permit issued under section 4, a permit referred to in section 4(h)(2), or the exemption contained in section 4(g)(1).

(b) No person may sell, purchase, exchange, transport, receive, or offer to sell, purchase, or exchange any archaeological resource if such resource was excavated or removed from public lands or Indian lands in violation of—

(1) the prohibition contained in subsection (a), or

(2) any provision, rule, regulation, ordinance, or permit in effect under any other provision of Federal law.

(c) No person may sell, purchase, exchange, transport, receive, or offer to sell, purchase, or exchange, in interstate or foreign commerce, any archaeological resource excavated, removed, sold, purchased, exchanged, transported, or received in violation of any provision, rule, regulation, ordinance, or permit in effect under State or local law.

(d) Any person who knowingly violates, or counsels, procures, solicits, or employs any other person to violate, any prohibition contained in subsection (a), (b), or (c) of this section shall, upon conviction, be fined not more than $10,000 or imprisoned for not more than one year, or both: provided, however, that if the commercial or archaeological value of the archaeological resources involved and the cost of restoration and repair of such resources exceeds the sum of $5,000, such person shall be fined not more than $20,000 or imprisoned not more than two years or both. In cases of a second or subsequent such violation upon conviction such person shall be fined not more than $100,000, or imprisoned not more than five years, or both.

(e) The prohibitions contained in this section shall take effect on the date of the enactment of this Act.

(f) Nothing in subsection (b) (1) of this section shall be deemed applicable to any person with respect to an archaeological resource which was in the lawful possession of such person prior to the date of the enactment of this Act.

(g) Nothing in subsection (d) of this section shall be deemed applicable to any person with respect to the removal of arrowheads located on the surface of the ground.

Civil Penalties

Section 7. (a) (1) Any person who violates any prohibition contained in an applicable regulation or permit issued under this Act may be assessed a civil penalty by the Federal land manager concerned. No penalty may be assessed under this subsection unless such person is given notice and opportunity for a hearing with respect to such violation. Each violation shall be a separate offense. Any such civil penalty may be remitted or mitigated by the Federal land manager concerned.

(2) The amount of such penalty shall be determined under regulations promulgated pursuant to this Act, taking into account, in addition to other factors—

(A) The archaeological or commercial value of the archaeological resource involved, and

(B) The cost of restoration and repair of the resource and the archaeological site involved.

Such regulations shall provide that, in the case of a second or subsequent violation by any person, the amount of such civil penalty may be double the amount which would have been assessed if such violation were the first by such person. The amount of any penalty assessed under this subsection for any violation shall not exceed an amount equal to double the cost of restoration and repair of resources and archaeological sites damaged and double the fair market value of resources destroyed or not recovered.

(3) No penalty shall be assessed under this section for the removal of arrowheads located on the surface of the ground.

(b) (1) Any person aggrieved by an order assessing a civil penalty under subsection (a) may file a petition for judicial review of such order with the United States District Court for the District of Columbia or for any other district in which such person resides or transacts business. Such petition may only be filed within the 30-day period beginning on the date the order making such assessment was issued. The court shall hear such action on the record made before the Federal land manager and shall sustain his action if it is supported by substantial evidence on the record considered as a whole.

(b) (2) If any person fails to pay an assessment of a civil penalty—

(A) after the order making the assessment has become a final order and such person has not filed a petition for judicial review of the order in accordance with paragraph (1), or

(B) after a court in an action brought under paragraph (1) has entered a final judgment upholding the assessment of a civil penalty, the Federal land manager may request the Attorney General to institute a civil action in a district court of the United States for any district in which such person is found, resides, or transacts business to collect the penalty and such court shall have jurisdiction to hear and decide any such action. In such action, the validity and amount of such penalty shall not be subject to review.

(C) Hearings held during the proceedings for the assessment of civil penalties authorized by subsection (a) shall be conducted in accordance with section 554 of title 5 of the United States Code. The Federal land manager may issue subpoenas for the attendance and testimony of witnesses and the production of relevant papers, books, and documents and administer oaths. Witnesses summoned shall be paid the same fees and mileage that are paid to witnesses in courts of the United States. In case of contumacy or failure to appear for any district in which such person is found or resides or transacts business, upon application by the United States and after notice to such person, shall have jurisdiction to issue an order requiring such person to appear and give testimony before the Federal land manager or to appear and produce documents before the Federal land manager, or both and any failure to obey such order of the court may be punished by such court as a contempt thereof.

Rewards; Forfeiture

Section 8. (a) Upon the certification of the Federal land manager concerned, the Secretary of the Treasury is directed to pay from the penalties and fines collected under sections 6 and 7 an amount equal to one-half of such penalty or fine, but not to exceed $500, to any person who furnishes information which leads to the finding of a civil violation, or the conviction of a criminal violation, with respect to which such penalty or fine was paid. If several persons provide such information, such amount shall be divided among such persons. No officer or employee of the United States or of any state or local government who furnishes information or renders service in the performance of his official duties shall be eligible for payment under this subsection.

(b) All archaeological resources with respect to which a violation of subsection (a), (b), or (c) or section 6 occurred and which are in the possession of any person, and all vehicles and equipment of any person which was used in connection with such violation, may be (in the discretion of the court or administrative law judge, as the case may be) subject to forfeiture to the United States upon—

(1) such person's conviction of such violation under section 6,

(2) assessment of a civil penalty against such person under section 7 with respect to such violation, or

(3) a determination by any court that such archaeological resources, vehicles, or equipment were involved in such violation.

(c) in cases in which the violation of the prohibition contained in subsection (a), (b), or (c) of section 6 involve archaeological resources excavated or removed from Indian lands, the Federal land manager or court, as the case may be, shall provide for payment to the Indian or Indian tribe involved of all penalties collected pursuant to section 7 and for transfer to such Indian or Indian tribe of all items forfeited under this section.

Confidentiality

Section 9. (a) Information concerning the nature and location of any archaeological resource for which the excavation or removal requires a permit under this Act or under any other provision of Federal law may not be made available to the public under subchapter II of chapter 5 of title 5 of the United States Code or under any other provision of law unless the Federal land manager concerned determines that such disclosure would—

(1) further the purposes of this Act or the Act of June 27, 1960 (16 U.S.C. 469-469c), and

(2) not create a risk of harm to such resources or to the site at which such resources are located.

(b) Notwithstanding the provisions of subsection (a), upon the written request of the Governor of any State, which request shall state—

(1) the specific site or area for which information is sought,

(2) the purpose for which such information is sought,

(3) a commitment by the Governor to adequately protect the confidentiality of such information to protect the resource from commercial exploitation.

The Federal land manager concerned shall provide to the Governor information concerning the nature and location or archaeological resources within the State of the requesting Governor.

Regulations; Intergovernmental Coordination

Section 10. (a) The Secretaries of the Interior, Agriculture, and Defense and the Chairman of the Board of the Tennessee Valley Authority, after consultation with the Federal land managers, Indian tribes representatives of concerned State agencies, and after public notice and hearing, shall promulgate such uniform rules and regulations as may be appropriate to carry out the purposes of this Act. Such rules and regulations may be promulgated only after consideration of the provisions of the American Indian Religious Freedom Act (92 Stat. 469; 42 U.S.C. 1966). Each uniform rule or regulation promulgated under this Act shall be submitted on the same calendar day to the Committee on Energy and Natural Resources of the United States Senate and to the Committee on Interior and Insular Affairs of the United States House of Representatives, and no such uniform rule or regulation may take effect before the expiration of a period of ninety calendar days following the date of its submission to such committees.

(b) Each Federal land manager shall promulgate such rules and regulations, consistent with the uniform rules and regulations under section (a), as may be appropriate for the carrying out of his functions and authorities under this Act.

Cooperation with Private Individuals

Section 11. The Secretary of the Interior shall take such action as may be necessary, consistent with the purposes of this Act, to foster and improve the communication, cooperation, and exchange of information between—

(1) private individuals having collections of archaeological resources and data which were obtained before the date of the enactment of this Act,

(2) Federal authorities responsible for the protection of archaeological resources on the public lands and Indian lands and professional archaeologists and associations of professional archaeologists.

In carrying out this section, the Secretary shall, to the extent practical and consistent with provisions of this Act, make efforts to expand the archaeological data base for the archaeological resources of the United States through increased cooperation between private individuals referred to in paragraph (1) and professional archaeologists and archaeological organizations.

Savings Provisions

Section 12. (a) Nothing in this Act shall be construed to repeal, modify, or impose additional restrictions on the activities permitted under existing laws and authorities relating to mining, mineral leasing, reclamation, and other multiple uses of the public lands.

(b) Nothing in this Act applies to, or requires a permit for, the collection for private purposes of any rock, coin, bullet, or mineral which is not an archaeological resource as determined under uniform regulations promulgated under section 3(1).

(c) Nothing in this Act shall be construed any land other than public land or Indian land or to effect the lawful recovery, collection or sale of archaeological resources from land other than public land or Indian land.

Report

Section 13. As part of the annual report required to be submitted to the specified committees of Congress pursuant to section 5(c) of the Act of June 27, 1960 (74 Stat. 220; 16 U.S.C. 469-469a), the Secretary of the Interior shall comprehensively report as a separate component on the activities carried out under the provisions of this Act, and he shall make such recommendations as he deems appropriate as to changes or improvements needed in the provisions of this Act. Such report shall include a brief summary of the actions undertaken by the Secretary under Section 11 of this Act, relating to cooperation with private individuals.

Approved October 31, 1979.

Index

199

*Ruins and sites recommended for visits